AF797869

Arrested for Drugs in Texas:

Your Step-by-Step Guide from Arrest to Moving Forward

By
Deandra M. Grant &
Douglas E. Huff

MEET THE AUTHORS

DEANDRA M. GRANT, JD, GC, MS

&

DOUGLAS E. HUFF, JD

Deandra M. Grant, JD, GC, MS

Deandra Grant was born in Denton but grew up in Plano and is a proud graduate of Plano Senior High School. A native Texan, her family has lived for generations in and around Gainesville, Texas.

Deandra's hard-nosed work ethic began at an early age with a variety of teenage jobs: social director at a teen nightclub, clerk at a dress shop and owner/manager of a New Orleans-style sno-cone stand (Mr Sno Ball!), to name a few.

After high school she attended Trinity University in San Antonio then came back home to Dallas for law school at SMU. Deandra has been married to Eric Clendenin for over 20 years and they have two children – Keegan and Rowan.

When not practicing law, she is very involved with dog rescue and serves as Vice President of Living the Doxie Dream Rescue & Sanctuary in Royse City. At home she and Eric have 5 rescue dachshunds and you can follow their adventures on their Instagram page @5WienerPack.

Deandra is a huge Van Halen fan (DLR – not Hagar), studies medieval European history as a hobby and loves to travel.

Lawyer Stuff:

Deandra was included in the list of Super Lawyers® for 2011- 2012, 2014 – present. Super Lawyers® is an attorney rating service that is nationally recognized throughout the legal community. After performing exhaustive and rigorous research by an independent research team, they announce their list of highly capable, trustworthy, and competent attorneys in Super Lawyers® Magazine and online. The list represents no more than 5% of the attorneys in Texas.

Deandra is AV® Preeminent ™ Rated by Martindale-Hubbell®, which is the highest rating an attorney can achieve. She was given the AV® Rating for her outstanding professional achievements in the field of DWI law and her contributions to the legal community. She's also been rated 10.0 by both AVVO and Justia.

Deandra began work on The Texas DWI Manual in 2011 for James Publishing. She calls it her "labor of love". The first edition was released in 2013. It is updated annually and is considered a "must have" for attorneys defending DWI cases in Texas.

Experience:

Deandra graduated in 1990 from Trinity University in San Antonio with a B.S. in Business Administration. She earned her law degree from the SMU School of Law and was licensed by the State Bar of Texas in 1993. Having spent her last year of law school as an intern with the Dallas County District Attorney's Office, she began work there as an assistant district attorney in January 1994.

Deandra's tenure as a prosecutor focused on DWI prosecution. In 1995, she founded her own firm and began defending citizens accused of DWI and other crimes. She has practiced criminal defense for over 30 years and represents Texans charged with criminal offenses, including

DWI, violent felonies, and sex crimes. As a former prosecutor, she knows firsthand how to counter the prosecutor's evidence and strategy.

Operator and Testing Experience:

Deandra has spent hundreds of hours in training courses and programs related to DWI defense. She has participated in numerous "dosing" experiments in which people are given specific amounts of alcohol over certain time periods and then tested to see the effect of the alcohol on their mental and physical capabilities. She attended and successfully completed the operator certification course for the Intoxilyzer 5000 in Florida in 2004. This was the breath-test machine used in Texas prior to the purchase of the Intoxilyzer 9000. She learned how to operate the machine and the science behind it. She has also participated in experiments related to the inaccuracy of the machine.

Deandra has completed both the student course (2008) and the instructor course (2009) on the administration of standardized field sobriety testing (SFST's), the same National Highway Traffic Safety Administration training course that teaches police officers nationwide how to identify drunk drivers during traffic stops. She now serves as an instructor of the SFST practitioner course to share the knowledge with other attorneys. In 2008, she completed coursework in Atlanta, Georgia on DWI forensic blood and urine testing.

In 2011, she began training at Axion Labs in Chicago. The courses include Forensic Chromatography, Forensic Drug Analysis and Forensic Driving Under the Influence of Drugs. She completed the coursework, passed the final exam in 2015 and was awarded the American Chemical Society Forensic Lawyer-Scientist Designation. In 2018 Deandra joined Axion Labs as an assistant chromatography instructor. She spends 5 weeks each year in Chicago at the lab.

In 2014 Deandra "went back to school". She completed a Graduate Certificate in Forensic Toxicology from the University of Florida's College of Veterinary Medicine and a Master's Degree in Pharmaceutical Science – Concentration in Forensic Science from the University of Florida's College of Pharmacy in 2016.

Deandra is a national speaker and teacher on topics including trial skills, jury selection, cross examination, field sobriety tests, drugged driving and forensic breath and blood alcohol testing. Since 2019 she's been honored to serve on the faculty of the Robert F. Borkenstein Course on the Effects of Drugs on Human Performance and Behavior.

Douglas E. Huff, JD

Attorney Douglas Huff was born in Warren, Ohio and was raised in Western Pennsylvania, outside of Pittsburgh, where he attended Mount Pleasant Area High School. After high school, Attorney Huff enlisted in the United States Army and served for four years receiving the Army Achievement Medal and the Army Commendation Medal. He received an honorable discharge after completing his full term of service and relocated to Austin, Texas.

After attending law school, Attorney Huff worked at Barbri, an organization specializing in assisting law students in studying and passing the state bar examination. In addition to being licensed to practice law in the state of Texas, he sat and passed the Oklahoma Bar during this time. Afterwards, he opened his own law practice, The Law Office of Douglas E. Huff in Dallas, Texas where he represented clients charged with various misdemeanor and felony criminal offenses.

In 2013, Attorney Huff accepted a position with the Dallas County Public Defender's Office where he worked diligently as the lead attorney in many DWI trials and other misdemeanors. Additionally, he has assisted numerous clients through plea negotiations, led many evidentiary hearings, and prepared and took part in felony trials.

Attorney Huff joined Deandra Grant Law in 2016. He became a partner in 2021. Doug is based in the Dallas office but practices throughout Texas.

On a personal note, Doug has one daughter (attorney Sorsha Huff) and a rescue dog named "Athena". He's a military vet who loves to travel. One of his favorite trips was walking the Camino de Santiago in Spain. Doug is also a competitive poker player you can often find playing in tournaments around the country.

TABLE OF CONTENTS

MEET NANCY:

Your Guide Through the Texas Criminal Justice System

Nancy is a 34-year-old registered nurse living in suburban Texas with her husband Mike and their two children, ages 8 and 12. After suffering a back injury at work, Nancy underwent surgery and was prescribed oxycontin for pain management. What started as legitimate medical treatment gradually became dependency, and when her prescription ended, Nancy found herself buying pills to avoid withdrawal symptoms.

A few months earlier, Nancy had received a speeding ticket but forgot to take care of it in the chaos of managing her addiction and family responsibilities. The unpaid ticket resulted in an arrest warrant being issued. During another traffic stop for speeding, the officer discovered the outstanding warrant and arrested Nancy. During the search incident to arrest, police found four oxycontin pills in her pocket - pills she didn't have a prescription for.

Nancy was charged with possession of a controlled substance (Penalty Group 1, less than one gram) - a state jail felony in Texas. As a first-time offender, Nancy is terrified about going to jail, losing her nursing license, and what this means for her family's future.

Nancy's story represents thousands of Texans who never imagined they'd face drug charges. She's not a "criminal" in the traditional sense - she's a healthcare professional, mother, and community member whose medical treatment led to addiction and a moment of poor judgment that changed her life.

Throughout this guidebook, you'll follow Nancy's journey through each step of the criminal justice process. You'll see how she navigates bail, finds an attorney, explores treatment options, and ultimately resolves her case. Her experiences will show you what to expect and help you understand your own options when facing similar charges.

CHAPTER 1: WHAT HAPPENS After a Drug Arrest in Texas

The moment the handcuffs clicked shut, Nancy's world turned upside down. One minute she was a working mother rushing to pick up her kids from school, the next she was sitting in the back of a police car, watching her life crumble through the rear window. The officer's words echoed in her mind: "You're under arrest for possession of a controlled substance."

If you're reading this chapter, you're probably feeling the same shock, fear, and disbelief that Nancy experienced. Maybe you're still in jail waiting for bond, or perhaps you've been released but can't stop replaying the arrest in your mind. Either way, you're scared about what comes next, and that's completely understandable. Being arrested for drug charges - especially when you never thought of yourself as a "criminal" - is one of the most overwhelming experiences a person can face.

Let me be clear about something important: this feeling of panic is normal and it will pass. You're not going crazy, you're not weak, and you're not a bad person. You're a good person who made a mistake or found yourself in a difficult situation. That doesn't change who you are at your core.

You're not alone in this journey, and what you're feeling right now is normal. Thousands of Texans go through this process every year, including nurses like Nancy, teachers, parents, students, and working professionals who found themselves in circumstances they never imagined. **Your life is not over.** This is a chapter in your story, not the final page.

This chapter will walk you through exactly what happens after a drug arrest in Texas, so you know what to expect and can start making informed decisions about your future.

🚨 IF YOU JUST GOT ARRESTED - READ THIS FIRST

What to Do RIGHT NOW:

- ☐ **Call an attorney TODAY** - Don't wait, , just start calling
- ☐ **Stay silent** - Don't discuss your case with anyone except your lawyer
- ☐ **Don't panic** - Thousands of people get through this and rebuild their lives
- ☐ **Take care of basics** - Eat, sleep, call family for support
- ☐ **Read this chapter** - Then worry about the rest later

Your Timeline This Week:

- ☐ **Today/Tomorrow:** Find and hire an attorney
- ☐ **This Week:** Attorney reviews your case and explains options
- ☐ **Next Week:** Possible first court date (attorney will handle this)
- ☐ **This Month:** Strategy development and case planning

Don't Worry About Yet:

- ☐ Trial preparation (may never happen)
- ☐ Sentencing (many cases end differently)
- ☐ Appeals (cross that bridge if needed)
- ☐ Long-term consequences (focus on immediate steps first)

IMMEDIATE ACTION CHECKLIST

If You're Still in Custody:

- ☐ Remain silent - don't discuss your case with anyone except your attorney
- ☐ Make your phone calls strategically (family for bail, attorney for legal help)
- ☐ Cooperate with booking procedures but don't volunteer information
- ☐ Ask for medical attention if needed
- ☐ Follow all jail rules to avoid additional problems

If You've Been Released:

- ☐ Contact an attorney immediately
- ☐ Review and understand your bond conditions
- ☐ Begin documenting positive life circumstances
- ☐ Avoid social media posts about your case
- ☐ Start gathering character references

⚠ CRITICAL WARNING

All jail phone calls except those to your attorney are recorded and can be used as evidence against you. Never discuss your case, admit guilt, or talk about what happened on these calls.

THE IMMEDIATE AFTERMATH: WHAT HAPPENS RIGHT NOW

The Ride to Jail

After your arrest, you'll be transported to the local jail for booking. This ride can feel like the longest of your life, but try to stay calm and remember your rights. You have the right to remain silent, and you should use it. Officers may try to make small talk or ask seemingly innocent questions about your day, your job, or what happened. Don't engage in this conversation. Anything you say can and will be used against you later, even casual comments that seem harmless.

Nancy made this mistake. During her ride to jail, she tried to explain to the officer that the pills were for her back pain and that she'd just forgotten to get a new prescription. She thought being honest and cooperative would help her situation. Instead, those statements became evidence that she knew the pills were controlled substances and that she possessed them without a valid prescription.

What to do: Politely tell the officer, «I'm going to remain silent and would like to speak with an attorney.» Then stop talking. Don't explain, don't defend yourself, and don't try to convince them of your innocence. There will be time for that later with your lawyer.

The Booking Process

Once you arrive at the jail, you'll go through the booking process. This is administrative, not investigative, so you'll need to cooperate with basic identification procedures. Here's what to expect:

Personal Information: You'll be asked for your name, address, date of birth, and other identifying information. Answer these questions truthfully - they're not asking about your case, just who you are.

Fingerprints and Photos: You'll be fingerprinted and photographed (the infamous «mugshot»). This is standard procedure for everyone who's arrested.

Property Inventory: They'll take all your belongings and make a list of everything. This includes your wallet, phone, jewelry, and anything else you had on you. They'll write down every item, including any suspected drugs.

Medical Screening: Jail staff will ask about health problems, medications, and whether you're under the influence. Answer honestly - they need this information to keep you safe.

Clothing Exchange: You'll be given jail clothing and your personal clothes will be stored with your other property.

Your First Phone Calls

After booking, you'll be allowed to make phone calls. Use these wisely:

Call 1: Family or Friends - Let someone know where you are and that you need help with bail. Give them the jail's information and your booking number.

Call 2: An Attorney - If you know a criminal defense lawyer, call them immediately. If you don't, ask family or friends to start looking for one.

Call 3: Your Employer - You may need to call in sick or make arrangements for missed work. Keep this conversation brief and don't discuss your case.

Important: All jail phone calls except those to your attorney are recorded and can be used as evidence. Don't discuss your case, don't admit guilt, and don't talk about what happened. Stick to logistics only.

UNDERSTANDING YOUR RIGHTS

Even though you've been arrested, you still have important constitutional rights that protect you throughout this process:

The Right to Remain Silent

This is your most important right, and you should use it from the moment of arrest until you speak with an attorney. Police may try various tactics to get you to talk:

- "Just tell us your side of the story"
- "This is your chance to explain what really happened"
- "Cooperation will look good for you in court"
- "We already know what happened, so you might as well admit it"

None of these statements are true. Your silence cannot be used against you, but your words absolutely can be. There is no benefit to talking to police without an attorney present, even if you're completely innocent.

The Right to an Attorney

You have the right to have an attorney present during any questioning. If you can't afford an attorney, one will be appointed for you. Don't wait to exercise this right - ask for a lawyer immediately and repeatedly if necessary.

The Right to a Phone Call

You're entitled to make phone calls to arrange for bail and to contact an attorney. Don't waste these calls discussing your case with family members.

The Right to Medical Care

If you need medical attention, you have the right to receive it while in custody. This is especially important if you're dealing with withdrawal symptoms or have other medical conditions.

DEALING WITH SHAME AND FAMILY IMPACT

What to Tell Your Family

For Your Spouse/Partner:

- Be honest about what happened without overwhelming them with details
- Focus on what you're doing to handle the situation
- Ask for their support and patience during this process
- Reassure them that you're getting professional help

For Your Children:

- Age-appropriate honesty is usually best
- Young children: "Mommy/Daddy made a mistake and has to work with some people to fix it"
- Teenagers: More detailed explanation focusing on learning and growth
- Emphasize that this doesn't change how much you love them

For Your Parents:

- They may be disappointed, but most parents want to help
- Focus on your plan for moving forward
- Ask for emotional support, not necessarily financial help
- Give them time to process their emotions

Managing Shame and Embarrassment

Remember:

- Everyone makes mistakes - this doesn't define you
- Many successful people have overcome similar challenges
- Your worth as a person isn't determined by your worst moment
- Focus on how you respond to this crisis, not the crisis itself

Practical Steps:

- Limit social media use if it increases anxiety
- Avoid people who make you feel worse about yourself
- Connect with supportive friends and family
- Consider counseling to process your emotions
- Focus on actions you can take rather than dwelling on regret

FINANCIAL REALITY: WHAT THIS WILL COST

Typical Total Costs for Drug Cases

ATTORNEY FEES:	AND FINES:	OTHER POTENTIAL COSTS:
Simple possession cases: $3,500-$7,500	Court costs: $300-$500	Bail/bond fees: 10-15% of bond amount
More complex cases: $5,000-$15,000+	Fines: $500-$10,000 (depending on charge)	Treatment programs: $500-$3,000
Payment plans available with most attorneys	Probation fees: $60/month if you get probation	Community service supervision: $50-$100
Court-appointed counsel available if you qualify	Drug testing fees: $25-$50 per test	Lost wages from court dates and jail time

$15,000+ depending on your case

IF YOU CAN'T AFFORD AN ATTORNEY
You Have Options:

- Apply for court-appointed counsel at your first court date
- Many attorneys offer payment plans
- Some attorneys take credit cards
- Family members can help with legal fees
- Legal aid organizations may assist

Don't Go Without a Lawyer: The cost of poor representation or self-representation is usually much higher than attorney fees.

WHAT'S HAPPENING BEHIND THE SCENES

While you're sitting in jail wondering what's next, several things are happening that will affect your case:

The Police Investigation Continues

Your arrest doesn't end the investigation - it often kicks it into high gear. Police may be:

- Applying for search warrants for your home, car, or phone
- Interviewing witnesses
- Following up on leads from your arrest
- Preparing evidence for the district attorney's office

This is why it's crucial not to discuss your case on recorded jail phone lines. You might inadvertently give investigators information they can use to build a stronger case against you.

The District Attorney Reviews Your Case

Within a few days, prosecutors will review the police reports and evidence to decide what charges to file. This is called filing a complaint. The charges you end up with may be different from what you were arrested for, depending on what the evidence shows.

Bond is Set

If you weren't released on a personal recognizance bond (essentially a promise to appear in court), a magistrate or judge will set a bail amount. This usually happens within 24-48 hours of your arrest. The amount depends on several factors:

- The severity of the charges
- Your criminal history
- Your ties to the community
- Whether you're considered a flight risk
- Public safety concerns

TIMELINE: WHAT HAPPENS WHEN

Understanding the timeline can help reduce your anxiety about the unknown:

First 24 Hours:

- Booking and processing
- Initial medical screening
- Bond amount set
- First opportunity to post bail

24-72 Hours:

- Formal charges may be filed by prosecutor
- Arraignment scheduled
- Attorney appointed if you can't afford one
- Bond conditions established

First Week:

- Attorney begins investigating your case
- Initial court appearance scheduled
- Discovery process begins

First Month:

- Pretrial motions may be filed
- Plea negotiations may begin
- Case management hearings

COMMON MISTAKES PEOPLE MAKE

Learning from others' mistakes can help you avoid making your situation worse:

Talking Too Much

Nancy's biggest regret was trying to explain herself to the arresting officer. "I thought if I was honest and cooperative, they'd see this was all a misunderstanding," she later said. "Instead, I gave them everything they needed to convict me."

Posting About the Case on Social Media

Your social media accounts may be monitored after your arrest. Don't post anything about your case, your feelings about police, or your legal strategy. Even posts that seem supportive ("Thanks for all the prayers during this difficult time") can be twisted by prosecutors.

Discussing the Case with Other Inmates

Jailhouse conversations are not confidential, and other inmates may try to use information about your case to help themselves. Don't trust anyone in jail with details about your situation.

Waiting Too Long to Get an Attorney

The sooner you have legal representation, the better. Evidence disappears, witnesses move away, and police memories fade. Early intervention by an attorney can sometimes prevent charges from being filed at all.

TAKING CARE OF YOURSELF

Being arrested is traumatic, and it's important to take care of your physical and mental health during this difficult time:

If You're Still in Custody

- Follow all jail rules to avoid additional problems
- Take advantage of any programs or services offered
- Stay in contact with family and friends (but not about your case)
- Begin thinking about your legal defense

If You've Been Released

- Comply with all bond conditions strictly
- Begin documenting your life - work history, community involvement, family responsibilities
- Consider counseling or treatment if substance abuse played a role in your arrest
- Start gathering character references

SIDEBAR: KEY TERMS

BOOKING:

The administrative process of recording your arrest, taking fingerprints and photos, and cataloging your property.

BOND/BAIL:

Money paid to secure your release from jail while your case is pending. You get this money back if you appear for all court dates.

ARRAIGNMENT:

Your first formal court appearance where you'll receive paperwork about your charges and may address bond issues.

DISCOVERY:

The legal process where your attorney obtains evidence from the prosecution, including police reports, lab results, and witness statements.

PERSONAL RECOGNIZANCE (PR) BOND:

Release from jail based on your promise to appear in court, without having to pay money upfront.

MAGISTRATE:

A judicial officer who can set bail and make other preliminary decisions in your case.

FREQUENTLY ASKED QUESTIONS

Q **Will my arrest show up on background checks even if I'm not convicted?**

A Arrest records are generally not public in Texas, but they may show up on certain types of background checks, especially for jobs requiring security clearances or professional licenses.

Q **Can I get my belongings back?**

A Personal property not related to your case will typically be returned when you're released. Property that's evidence may be held until your case is resolved.

Q **What if I was arrested but haven't been formally charged yet?**

A The prosecutor has a limited time to file formal charges. If they don't file within that time, you may be released. However, they can still file charges later if they develop additional evidence.

Q **Should I try to contact the victims or witnesses?**

A Absolutely not. Any contact with victims or witnesses can be charged as witness tampering or stalking, even if your intentions are innocent.

Q **Can I travel while my case is pending?**

A This depends on your bond conditions. Many bonds restrict travel outside certain counties. Always check with your attorney before making travel plans.

WHAT NANCY LEARNED

Looking back on her arrest experience, Nancy wishes she had known several things that would have made the process less traumatic:

"I wish I had understood that being arrested doesn't mean you're guilty, and it doesn't mean your life is over. I spent so much time panicking and feeling ashamed that I wasn't thinking clearly about what I needed to do to protect myself. The most important thing I learned is that you have to stop talking and start thinking strategically from the very first moment."

💡 **NANCY'S TIP**

"The hardest part was not knowing what to expect. Once I understood that arrest is just the beginning of a process - not the end of my world - I could start thinking clearly about what I needed to do to protect myself and my family."

MOVING FORWARD

Your arrest is not the end of your story - it's the beginning of a legal process that you can navigate successfully with the right information and representation. The decisions you make in these first few days and weeks can significantly impact the outcome of your case.

Remember these key points as you move forward:

- Exercise your right to remain silent
- Get an attorney as soon as possible
- Follow all bond conditions strictly
- Document your positive life circumstances
- Don't discuss your case with anyone except your lawyer
- Take care of your physical and mental health

The road ahead may seem daunting, but thousands of people have walked this path before you and come out the other side with their lives intact. With the right approach and good legal representation, you can too.

IMPORTANT REMINDERS

- **Silence is your friend** - You cannot talk your way out of trouble, but you can definitely talk your way into more trouble
- **Time matters** - The sooner you get an attorney, the better they can protect your rights
- **Bond conditions are serious** - Violating them can land you back in jail and hurt your case
- **Document everything** - Start building a record of your positive life circumstances now

In the next chapter, we'll help you understand exactly what charges you're facing and what the potential penalties might be. Knowledge is power, and the more you understand about your situation, the better equipped you'll be to make smart decisions about your defense.

CHAPTER 2:

UNDERSTANDING YOUR DRUG CHARGES AND PENALTIES

When Nancy first heard the officer say "possession of a controlled substance," she had no idea what that actually meant. Was it a misdemeanor? A felony? What kind of punishment was she looking at? The legal paperwork she received was full of confusing terms like "Penalty Group 1" and "state jail felony" that might as well have been written in a foreign language.

Here's the thing about drug charges in Texas - they're not all created equal. The penalties you're facing depend on a bunch of different factors: what type of drug it was, how much you had, where you were when you got caught, and whether you've been in trouble before. It's kind of like a complicated recipe where each ingredient changes the final outcome.

I know this stuff can feel overwhelming, especially when you're already stressed about everything else going on. But understanding exactly what you're charged with is crucial for making smart decisions about your case. Think of this chapter as your translation guide for all that legal jargon. We'll break down how Texas organizes drug crimes, what the different penalty groups mean, and what kind of punishment ranges you might be looking at. By the end, you'll understand your charges as well as your lawyer does.

📖 IF YOU ONLY READ ONE THING IN THIS CHAPTER

Find your charge on the quick reference guide below, then focus on the punishment range section. Everything else is helpful but not essential right now. The most important thing is understanding what you're actually facing so you can evaluate any plea offers or attorney advice you receive.

QUICK REFERENCE: IS YOUR CHARGE A MISDEMEANOR OR FELONY?

Misdemeanors (Less Serious):

- ☐ Marijuana possession under 4 ounces
- ☐ Small amounts of synthetic marijuana (under 2 ounces)
- ☐ Drug paraphernalia possession
- ☐ Small amounts of certain prescription drugs (under specific weight thresholds)

Felonies (More Serious):

- ☐ Any amount of cocaine, heroin, methamphetamine, ecstasy
- ☐ Larger amounts of prescription drugs without a valid prescription
- ☐ Marijuana over 4 ounces
- ☐ Any delivery or manufacturing charges

HOW TEXAS ORGANIZES DRUG CRIMES

Texas doesn't just throw all drugs into one big category. Instead, the law divides controlled substances into different "penalty groups" based on their potential for abuse and medical value. Think of it like organizing a library - similar books go on the same shelf, and similar drugs get similar punishments.

Penalty Group 1: The "Hard Drugs"

This group includes the substances Texas considers most dangerous:

Common Drugs in This Group:

- Cocaine and crack cocaine
- Heroin and other opiates
- Methamphetamine
- LSD
- Oxycontin, Percocet, and other prescription opioids (without a prescription)
- Fentanyl

Why Nancy's Case Was So Serious: Nancy's oxycontin pills fell into Penalty Group 1, which is why she was facing felony charges even though she only had four pills. Texas doesn't mess around with these substances.

Penalty Group 1-A: Designer Drugs

This newer category covers:

- LSD (moved here from Penalty Group 1)
- Certain synthetic drugs

The penalties are similar to Penalty Group 1, but the weight measurements are different.

Penalty Group 2: "Club Drugs" and Hallucinogens

Common Drugs in This Group:

- Ecstasy (MDMA)
- PCP
- Amphetamines (like Adderall without a prescription)
- Mescaline
- Certain prescription stimulants

Penalty Group 3: Prescription Drugs

Common Drugs in This Group:

- Valium, Xanax, and other benzodiazepines
- Ritalin and other ADHD medications
- Certain prescription painkillers
- Anabolic steroids

Penalty Group 4: Prescription Drugs with Lower Abuse Potential

Common Drugs in This Group:

- Certain prescription medications with limited street value
- Some compounds containing small amounts of controlled substances

Marijuana: Its Own Category

Marijuana gets special treatment under Texas law and isn't grouped with other drugs. The penalties depend solely on the amount you possessed.

NANCY'S DISCOVERY

"I had no idea that prescription pills were treated the same as street drugs. I thought because a doctor had originally prescribed them to me, somehow that would matter. My lawyer explained that once my prescription ran out, those pills became illegal controlled substances, just like if I'd been caught with cocaine."

UNDERSTANDING POSSESSION VS. DELIVERY

The amount of drugs you're caught with doesn't just determine how severe your punishment might be - it can completely change what crime you're charged with.

Simple Possession

This is exactly what it sounds like: having drugs for your own personal use. Nancy was charged with simple possession because she had four pills that were clearly for personal consumption.

Key Point: You can be charged with possession even if the drugs aren't technically «yours.» If they're in your car, your house, or your pocket, you can be charged with possessing them.

Possession with Intent to Deliver

If prosecutors think you planned to sell or give away the drugs, the charges become much more serious. They don't need to catch you in the act of selling - they can infer intent from circumstances like:

- Large quantities of drugs
- Multiple small baggies or containers
- Scales or measuring devices
- Large amounts of cash
- Text messages about selling drugs
- Multiple cell phones

Real Example: Maria, Nancy's coworker, was caught with 20 oxycontin pills. Even though she said they were all for her personal use because of severe chronic pain, prosecutors charged her with intent to deliver because of the quantity. Her penalty range jumped from 2 years maximum to 20 years maximum.

Manufacturing and Delivery

These are the most serious drug charges and involve actually making or selling controlled substances. Even giving drugs away for free counts as "delivery" under Texas law.

SIDEBAR: KEY TERMS

PENALTY GROUP:

Texas's system for categorizing drugs based on their potential for abuse and accepted medical use.

USABLE QUANTITY:

The amount of drug needed to support a possession charge. It must be a measurable amount that could actually be used.

AGGREGATE WEIGHT:

For pills and other preparations, Texas weighs the entire pill or liquid, not just the pure drug inside it. So a heavy pill with a little bit of drug gets treated the same as a lighter pill with more drug.

ENHANCEMENT:

Legal mechanism that increases your punishment because of prior convictions. Think of it as the system saying «You've been here before, so this time is worse.»

DRUG-FREE ZONE:

Areas around schools, playgrounds, and youth centers where drug penalties are increased.

PUNISHMENT RANGES: WHAT YOU'RE ACTUALLY LOOKING AT

Now for the part you're probably most worried about - what kind of punishment are you facing? Texas has specific ranges for each type of drug offense, and understanding these ranges helps you evaluate plea offers and make informed decisions.

Marijuana Penalties

Under 2 Ounces (Class B Misdemeanor):

- Up to 180 days in jail
- Up to $2,000 fine
- Eligible for probation

2-4 Ounces (Class A Misdemeanor):

- Up to 1 year in jail
- Up to $4,000 fine
- Eligible for probation

4 Ounces to 5 Pounds (State Jail Felony):

- 180 days to 2 years in state jail
- Up to $10,000 fine
- Eligible for probation

5-50 Pounds (3rd Degree Felony):

- 2-10 years in prison
- Up to $10,000 fine
- Eligible for probation

Penalty Group 1 (Nancy's Situation)

Under 1 Gram (State Jail Felony):

- 180 days to 2 years in state jail
- Up to $10,000 fine
- Eligible for probation (if first felony)

1-4 Grams (3rd Degree Felony):

- 2-10 years in prison
- Up to $10,000 fine
- Eligible for probation

4-200 Grams (2nd Degree Felony):

- 2-20 years in prison
- Up to $10,000 fine
- Eligible for probation

200-400 Grams (1st Degree Felony):

- 5-99 years in prison
- Up to $10,000 fine
- Eligible for probation

Penalty Groups 2, 3, and 4

These follow similar patterns but with slightly different weight thresholds. Generally, the punishment ranges are the same as Penalty Group 1 for similar amounts.

⚠ CRITICAL UNDERSTANDING

Eligible for probation doesn't mean you'll automatically get probation. It means the law allows the judge to sentence you to probation instead of jail or prison time. Many factors influence whether you actually receive probation.

FACTORS THAT CAN INCREASE YOUR PENALTIES

Several circumstances can make your situation more serious and increase the punishment you're facing:

Prior Criminal History

Previous Drug Convictions: If you have prior drug convictions, even misdemeanors, your punishment range can be enhanced significantly. A second felony drug conviction can bump you up to the next penalty level.

Other Felony Convictions: Previous felonies, even non-drug related, can be used to enhance your punishment. Two prior felonies can make you eligible for life imprisonment under Texas's habitual offender laws.

Drug-Free Zones

If you were arrested within 1,000 feet of certain locations, your charges can be enhanced:

- Schools and school buses
- Playgrounds
- Youth centers
- Public swimming pools
- Video arcade facilities

How This Affects Penalties: Being in a drug-free zone can bump a misdemeanor up to a felony or increase the punishment range for felony charges.

Real Example: Tom was arrested with a small amount of marijuana (normally a Class B misdemeanor) while parked near his child's elementary school. Because he was in a drug-free zone, his charge was enhanced to a Class A misdemeanor, doubling his potential jail time.

Weapons

Having a weapon during a drug offense can lead to additional charges and increased penalties, even if the weapon was legally owned and you never threatened anyone with it.

SPECIAL CONSIDERATIONS FOR PRESCRIPTION DRUGS

Since many people facing drug charges were originally prescribed the medications legally, it's important to understand how prescription drugs are treated:

When Prescription Drugs Become Illegal

- **After your prescription expires:** Once your prescription runs out, any remaining pills become illegal controlled substances
- **Sharing with others:** Giving your prescribed medication to anyone else is illegal delivery
- **Getting from multiple doctors:** «Doctor shopping» to get multiple prescriptions is illegal
- **Buying from others:** Purchasing prescription drugs from anyone other than a licensed pharmacy is illegal possession

The "Prescription Defense"

Having an old prescription bottle doesn't protect you if:

- The prescription has expired
- You have more pills than the prescription allowed
- The pills are a different type than what was prescribed
- You can't prove the pills came from that prescription

CHARGE EVALUATION CHECKLIST

UNDERSTANDING YOUR SPECIFIC SITUATION:

- [ ] What penalty group is your drug in?
- [ ] How much did you allegedly possess?
- [ ] Are you charged with possession, intent to deliver, or delivery?
- [ ] Do you have any prior convictions that could enhance your charges?
- [ ] Were you arrested in a drug-free zone?
- [ ] Are there any weapons charges?
- [ ] What's the maximum punishment you're facing?
- [ ] Are you eligible for probation?

COMMON MISCONCEPTIONS

Let's clear up some myths that can hurt your case:

"It's Just a Small Amount"

The amount matters for determining your punishment range. Very small amounts of some prescription drugs might only be misdemeanors, but any usable quantity of Penalty Group 1 substances like cocaine, heroin, or methamphetamine will typically result in felony charges.

"It's My First Offense"

Being a first-time offender helps with getting probation, but it doesn't make felony charges go away or automatically guarantee a light sentence.

"I Have a Medical Condition"

Having a legitimate medical need for controlled substances doesn't legalize possessing them without a valid prescription.

"I Didn't Know They Were Illegal"

Ignorance of the law isn't a defense. You're expected to know that possessing controlled substances without a prescription is illegal.

💡 UNDERSTANDING PLEA NEGOTIATIONS

Knowing your potential punishment range is crucial for evaluating plea offers. If you're facing 2-20 years for a 2nd degree felony, an offer to plead to a state jail felony (maximum 2 years) might look pretty good. But if you're only facing 180 days to 2 years anyway, that same offer isn't much of a deal.

HOW YOUR CHARGES AFFECT OTHER AREAS OF YOUR LIFE

Understanding your charges isn't just about potential jail time - drug convictions can affect many other aspects of your life:

Professional Licenses

Different types of charges affect professional licenses differently. A misdemeanor marijuana charge might not end your career, but a felony involving prescription drugs could be devastating for healthcare professionals.

Immigration Status

Any controlled substance conviction, even a misdemeanor, can have serious immigration consequences. The specific charge and penalty group matter enormously for non-citizens.

Employment

Many employers have different policies for misdemeanors vs. felonies, and some care more about drug charges than other types of crimes.

Housing

Felony drug convictions can make it difficult to rent apartments or qualify for certain types of housing assistance.

FREQUENTLY ASKED QUESTIONS

Q **Can charges be reduced through plea negotiations?**

A Yes, prosecutors often offer reduced charges in exchange for guilty pleas. Understanding your current charges helps you evaluate whether a proposed reduction is worthwhile.

Q **What if I was charged with the wrong penalty group?**

A This happens sometimes, especially with prescription drugs. Your attorney can challenge the classification if the substance was misidentified.

Q **Do enhanced charges have to be proven at trial?**

A Yes, any enhancements (prior convictions, drug-free zones, etc.) must be proven beyond a reasonable doubt, just like the underlying charge.

Q **Can I be charged with possession if the drugs belonged to someone else?**

A Yes, if you had knowledge of the drugs and control over them. This is called «constructive possession» and is just as serious as actual possession.

WHAT NANCY WISHES SHE'D KNOWN

"I spent the first few weeks after my arrest in complete panic because I didn't understand what I was actually facing. Once my lawyer explained that my charge was a state jail felony with a maximum of 2 years, and that first-time offenders usually get probation, I could finally think clearly about my options. I wish I'd understood from day one that my situation, while serious, wasn't the end of the world."

Moving Forward with Knowledge

Now that you understand the basics of how Texas categorizes drug charges and what penalties you might be facing, you're better equipped to:

- Evaluate plea offers from prosecutors
- Understand your attorney's strategy recommendations
- Make informed decisions about going to trial
- Prepare for sentencing if you're convicted
- Plan for how this charge might affect other areas of your life

Remember, being charged with a crime doesn't mean you'll be convicted, and being convicted doesn't mean you'll receive the maximum punishment. Understanding your charges is the first step toward building an effective defense and achieving the best possible outcome for your situation.

In the next chapter, we'll walk you through your first court appearance - the arraignment - so you know exactly what to expect when you walk into that courtroom.

CHAPTER 3:

YOUR FIRST COURT DATE - ARRAIGNMENT EXPLAINED

Nancy stared at the court notice in her hands, her heart racing as she read the date and time for her arraignment. She'd never been inside a courtroom before, and the thought of facing a judge terrified her. What would she say? What would happen? Would they send her straight to jail?

Here's what Nancy - and you - need to know: arraignment is not the scary, life-changing courtroom drama you see on TV. It's actually a pretty straightforward administrative process, and you're going to get through it just fine. Thousands of people walk into Texas courtrooms every day for their arraignments, and they walk right back out. This is just the first step in your legal journey, not the final destination.

You have rights during this process, and the system is designed to protect those rights. You don't need to have all the answers today, you don't need to defend yourself, and you certainly don't need to figure out your entire case before walking into that courtroom. Your job is simply to show up, listen, and take the next appropriate step. This chapter will prepare you for exactly what to expect, what questions you might be asked, and how to handle yourself with confidence. By the time you finish reading, you'll walk into that courtroom knowing exactly what's going to happen.

ARRAIGNMENT DAY CHECKLIST

Before You Leave Home:

- ☐ Dress appropriately (business casual, no shorts, flip-flops, or revealing clothing)
- ☐ Bring your court notice and ID
- ☐ Arrive 30 minutes early to find parking and get through security
- ☐ Turn off your cell phone before entering the courtroom
- ☐ Bring contact information for family/friends in case you need bail help

What NOT to Bring:

- ☐ Weapons of any kind (including pocket knives)
- ☐ Large bags or purses (most courts have restrictions)
- ☐ Food or drinks
- ☐ Cameras or recording devices

UNDERSTANDING FORMAL VS. INFORMAL ARRAIGNMENTS

In Texas, there are two different ways your arraignment might happen, and understanding the difference will help you know what to expect.

Informal Arraignments (Most Common)

Most arraignments in Texas are handled administratively rather than in open court. Here's how it typically works:

Before Your Court Date: You may receive paperwork in the mail or when you were released from jail that includes:

- A copy of the formal charges against you
- Information about your rights
- Notice of your next court date
- Instructions about what to do next

At the Court: You'll likely check in with a clerk or court coordinator who will:

- Verify that you received the charging documents
- Confirm your contact information
- Explain your next court date
- Help you apply for court-appointed counsel if needed

Nancy's Experience: «I was so nervous about my arraignment, but when I got to court, I just checked in with a clerk who handed me some paperwork and told me my next court date. The whole thing took about five minutes, and I never even saw the inside of a courtroom.»

Formal Arraignments (Less Common)

Some cases, particularly more serious felonies or when you're still in custody, may require a formal arraignment in front of a judge. Here's what happens:

In the Courtroom: You'll appear before a judge who will:

- Read the charges against you aloud
- Explain the potential penalties you're facing
- Inform you of your constitutional rights
- Ask if you understand the charges and your rights
- Address any bail or bond issues if you're still in custody

Your Role: You'll be asked to confirm that you understand the charges and your rights. You're not entering a plea at this stage - that comes later.

IMPORTANT REMINDER

You do NOT enter a plea at arraignment in Texas. Despite what you see on TV, Texas arraignments are about informing you of the charges and your rights, not about pleading guilty or not guilty. That happens at a later court setting.

YOUR CONSTITUTIONAL RIGHTS

Whether your arraignment is formal or informal, you'll be informed of your constitutional rights. Understanding these rights is crucial for protecting yourself throughout the legal process.

Right to an Attorney

You have the absolute right to be represented by an attorney at every stage of your case. This includes:

- **If you can afford an attorney:** You can hire any licensed criminal defense lawyer
- **If you cannot afford an attorney:** The court will appoint counsel to represent you
- **Right to adequate time:** You have the right to reasonable time to find and consult with an attorney before making any major decisions

Right to Remain Silent

You have the right to remain silent and not incriminate yourself. This means:

- You don't have to testify at your trial
- You don't have to answer questions from police or prosecutors
- Your silence cannot be used against you as evidence of guilt

Right to Trial by Jury

You have the right to have your case decided by a jury of your peers, which includes:

- **For felonies:** A jury of 12 people who must reach a unanimous verdict
- **For misdemeanors:** A jury of 6 people who must reach a unanimous verdict

- **Waiver option:** You can waive jury trial only if both you and the prosecutor agree to a bench trial

Right to Confront Witnesses

You have the right to cross-examine any witnesses who testify against you and to present witnesses on your own behalf.

Right to a Speedy Trial

You have the right to have your case resolved within a reasonable time frame.

SIDEBAR: KEY TERMS

ARRAIGNMENT:

The court proceeding where you're formally notified of the charges against you and informed of your rights.

COURT-APPOINTED COUNSEL:

An attorney paid by the county to represent defendants who cannot afford to hire their own lawyer.

PROBABLE CAUSE:

The standard of evidence needed to justify your arrest and formal charges.

BENCH TRIAL:

A trial decided by a judge rather than a jury.

WAIVER:

Giving up a right, such as the right to jury trial.

CONTINUANCE:

Postponing a court date to a later time.

WHAT HAPPENS WITH BAIL AND BOND

If you're still in custody when your arraignment occurs, addressing your bail situation will be a priority. If you've already been released, the judge may still review your bond conditions.

Setting or Reviewing Bail

Factors the Judge Considers:

- The severity of your charges
- Your criminal history
- Your ties to the community (job, family, residence)
- Whether you're considered a flight risk
- Public safety concerns
- Your ability to pay

Types of Bond:

- **Cash Bond:** You pay the full amount in cash
- **Surety Bond:** A bondsman posts bond for a fee (usually 10-15%)
- **Property Bond:** Real estate is used as collateral
- **Personal Recognizance:** Released on your promise to appear

Bond Conditions

The judge may impose conditions on your release, such as:

- Regular check-ins with a pretrial services officer
- No drug or alcohol use
- No contact with alleged victims or witnesses
- Staying within certain geographical boundaries
- Surrendering your passport
- No possession of weapons

NANCY'S INSIGHT

"I was already out on bond when my arraignment happened, so I thought it was just a formality. But my attorney explained that understanding my rights was actually the most important part. Knowing I had the right to remain silent and the right to an attorney helped me feel more confident about the whole process."

APPLYING FOR COURT-APPOINTED COUNSEL

If you cannot afford to hire an attorney, you can apply for court-appointed counsel during or after your arraignment.

Financial Eligibility

The court will evaluate your financial situation based on:

- Your income and employment status
- Your assets and property
- Your monthly expenses and debts
- The number of dependents you support

The Application Process

Complete Financial Affidavit: You'll fill out detailed paperwork about your finances. Be honest - providing false information can result in additional criminal charges.

Provide Documentation: You may need to bring:

- Pay stubs or proof of income
- Bank statements
- Tax returns
- Information about assets and debts

Court Review: A judge or magistrate will review your application and determine if you qualify for appointed counsel.

What to Expect from Court-Appointed Attorneys

Court-appointed attorneys in Texas are private lawyers who contract with counties to handle indigent defense cases. In some larger jurisdictions the county has a public defender's office from which they first appoint. They are:

- Licensed attorneys with the same qualifications as privately hired lawyers
- Experienced in criminal defense
- Bound by the same ethical obligations as all attorneys
- Required to provide competent representation

COMMON ARRAIGNMENT SCENARIOS

Scenario 1:
You're Out on Bond (Most Common)

What Happens:

- ☐ You check in with court staff
- ☐ Receive formal charging documents
- ☐ Get your next court date
- ☐ Apply for appointed counsel if needed
- ☐ Leave the courthouse

Time Required:

Usually 15-30 minutes

Scenario 2: You're Still in Custody

What Happens:

- ☐ You appear before a judge via video link or in person
- ☐ Judge reviews your charges and rights
- ☐ Bail is set or reviewed
- ☐ Attorney appointed if you qualify
- ☐ Next court date scheduled

Time Required:

Usually 30-60 minutes

Scenario 3: You Already Have an Attorney

What Happens:

- ☐ Your attorney may appear on your behalf
- ☐ You might not need to personally appear
- ☐ Attorney receives charging documents and discovery
- ☐ Next court date scheduled

Time Required: You may not need to attend at all

QUESTIONS TO ASK AT ARRAIGNMENT

About Your Case:

- [ ] What exactly am I charged with?
- [ ] When is my next court date?
- [ ] Do I need to be present at the next hearing?
- [ ] How do I get copies of the police reports and evidence?

About Representation:

- [ ] How do I apply for court-appointed counsel?
- [ ] When will an attorney be appointed?
- [ ] Can I hire my own attorney even after one is appointed?

About Bond Conditions:

- [ ] What are the specific conditions of my release?
- [ ] What happens if I violate bond conditions?
- [ ] Can bond conditions be modified?

COURTHOUSE ETIQUETTE AND WHAT TO EXPECT

Arriving at Court

Security: All courthouses have metal detectors and security screening. Allow extra time for this process.

Finding Your Courtroom: Court notices usually include specific courtroom numbers and directions. Ask courthouse staff if you're lost.

Check-In: Look for signs directing you to check in for arraignments or ask court staff where to go.

Courtroom Behavior

Stand When the Judge Enters: Everyone stands when the judge comes in and sits when told to do so.

Address the Judge Properly: Say «Your Honor» when speaking to the judge.

Speak Clearly: If asked a question, answer clearly and honestly.

Stay Quiet: Don't talk during other people's cases or make noise that disrupts proceedings.

No Cell Phones: Turn off your phone completely before entering the courtroom.

⚠ **CRITICAL WARNING**

Do NOT discuss your case while in the courthouse. Prosecutors, police officers, and other court personnel may overhear conversations that could hurt your case. Save all case discussions for private meetings with your attorney.

WHAT NOT TO DO AT ARRAIGNMENT

DON'T TRY TO ARGUE YOUR CASE

Arraignment is not the time to explain what happened or argue your innocence. That's what trials are for.

DON'T REPRESENT YOURSELF

Even if you plan to hire an attorney later, don't try to handle the arraignment on your own. If you qualify for appointed counsel, request it immediately.

DON'T IGNORE COURT ORDERS

If the judge gives you instructions or sets conditions, follow them exactly. Violation can result in additional charges and revocation of your bond.

DON'T MISS YOUR NEXT COURT DATE

Whatever you do, don't miss your next scheduled court appearance. This can result in a warrant for your arrest and forfeiture of any bond money.

AFTER YOUR ARRAIGNMENT: NEXT STEPS

If You Received Court-Appointed Counsel

- ☐ **Contact Your Attorney:** Call the appointed attorney's office within a few days to schedule a meeting.
- ☐ **Gather Documents:** Start collecting any documents that might help your case (medical records, employment records, character references).
- ☐ **Follow Bond Conditions:** Strictly comply with all conditions of your release.

If You're Hiring Your Own Attorney

- ☐ **Start Shopping:** Use the time between arraignment and your next court date to interview attorneys.
- ☐ **Ask for Recommendations:** Talk to friends, family, or other professionals for referrals.
- ☐ **Schedule Consultations:** Most criminal defense attorneys offer free initial consultations.

Preparing for Your Next Court Date

- ☐ **Mark Your Calendar:** Write down your next court date immediately and set multiple reminders.
- ☐ **Plan Ahead:** Arrange time off work and transportation to court.
- ☐ **Stay in Touch:** Keep your attorney informed of any changes in your contact information.

FREQUENTLY ASKED QUESTIONS

Q **What if I don't uWnderstand what the judge is saying?**

A Ask for clarification. Judges are used to explaining things, and it's important that you understand what's happening.

Q **Can I change my mind about court-appointed counsel later?**

A Yes, you can usually hire your own attorney even after one has been appointed, though there may be some procedural requirements.

Q **What if I miss my arraignment?**

A A warrant will likely be issued for your arrest. Contact an attorney immediately to help resolve the situation.

Q **Do I have to answer questions from prosecutors?**

A No, you have the right to remain silent. Any questioning should be done through your attorney.

Q **Can my family attend my arraignment?**

A Yes, most arraignments are public proceedings, and family members can attend for support.

WHAT NANCY LEARNED

"Looking back, I was so worried about my arraignment for nothing. I thought the judge was going to lecture me or that I'd have to defend myself in front of a room full of people. Instead, it was just a quick administrative process where I got information about my case and my rights. The most important thing I learned was that arraignment is just the beginning - it's where you get organized and prepared for what comes next, not where your case gets decided."

Moving Forward with Confidence

Your arraignment is a crucial step in your legal journey, but it's not something to fear. You now know:

- What to expect whether your arraignment is formal or informal
- Your constitutional rights and how they protect you
- How to apply for court-appointed counsel if needed
- Proper courthouse etiquette and behavior
- What questions to ask and what mistakes to avoid
- How to prepare for your next court appearance

Remember, the arraignment is just the beginning of your case, not the end. Use this opportunity to get organized, understand your rights, and start building your defense strategy with qualified legal counsel.

In the next chapter, we'll walk you through the bail and bond process, so you understand all your options for staying out of jail while your case is pending.

CHAPTER 4:

BAIL, BOND, AND GETTING OUT OF JAIL

When Nancy was arrested, her biggest fear wasn't the charges - it was the thought of staying in jail and missing work, leaving her kids wondering where mommy was. She needed to get home, but the bail amount seemed impossible to afford on a nurse's salary. The whole bond process felt like another obstacle designed to keep her locked up.

Let me be clear about something: getting out of jail on bond is not just possible, it's probable. The vast majority of people charged with drug offenses in Texas are released on bond while their cases work through the courts. The system recognizes that you have a life, a job, and responsibilities that don't stop just because you've been arrested. You're not stuck, and you're not helpless.

Yes, posting bond costs money, and yes, that can be stressful when you're already dealing with legal problems. But there are multiple ways to make it work, and you have more options than you probably realize. The key is understanding how the bond system operates, what your choices are, and how to make the smart financial decision for your situation. This chapter will give you that knowledge and put you back in control of your immediate future. By the time you're done reading, you'll know exactly how to get yourself home and back to your life while you fight your case.

BOND OPTIONS QUICK REFERENCE

Cash Bond:

- Pay full bail amount in cash
- Get money back when case ends (minus fees)
- Most expensive upfront, but least expensive long-term

Surety Bond (Bondsman):

- Pay 10-15% fee to bondsman
- Bondsman posts full amount
- Fee is non-refundable

Property Bond:

- Use real estate as collateral
- Property value must exceed bond amount
- No upfront cash required

Personal Recognizance (PR):

- Released on promise to appear
- No money required
- Only available for certain charges/circumstances

HOW BAIL IS SET IN TEXAS

Understanding how judges set bail amounts helps you know what to expect and how to potentially get a lower amount.

Factors Judges Consider

The Charges Against You:

- More serious charges typically mean higher bail
- Drug delivery charges usually have higher bail than simple possession
- Prior drug charges can increase bail amounts

Your Criminal History:

- First-time offenders typically get lower bail
- Prior failures to appear in court significantly increase bail
- Previous convictions, especially recent ones, raise bail amounts

Community Ties:

- Stable employment
- Family in the area
- Length of residence in the community
- Property ownership
- Community involvement

Flight Risk Assessment:

- Do you have ties outside the area?
- Do you have a passport?
- Are there pending charges in other jurisdictions?
- Have you missed court dates before?

Public Safety:

- Nature of the alleged offense
- Whether weapons were involved
- Perceived danger to specific individuals or the community

Financial Resources:

- Your ability to pay (though this shouldn't be the only factor)
- Assets and income
- Support from family and friends

NANCY'S EXPERIENCE

"My bail was set at $5,000, which felt like a fortune to me. But my attorney explained that for a first-time state jail felony, that was actually pretty reasonable. He helped me understand that I only needed $500 to get a bondsman, not the full $5,000."

YOUR BOND OPTIONS EXPLAINED

Cash Bond: Pay the Full Amount

How it Works: You or someone on your behalf pays the entire bail amount to the court in cash.

Advantages:

- No ongoing fees or interest
- You get the money back when your case ends (minus small administrative fees)
- No bondsman to deal with
- No additional conditions beyond what the court sets

Disadvantages:

- Requires having the full amount available immediately
- Money is tied up until your case ends (which could be months or years)
- If you miss court, you lose the entire amount

Best For: People who have access to the full bail amount and don't need that money for living expenses or attorney fees.

Nancy's Consideration: Nancy could have paid the full $5,000 cash bond using her savings, but her attorney advised against it. «You're going to need money for legal fees and living expenses if this drags out,» he told her. «Don't tie up all your cash in bond.»

Surety Bond: Using a Bondsman

How it Works: A licensed bail bondsman posts the full bond amount with the court. You pay the bondsman a fee (typically 10-15% of the total bond amount).

The Process:

1. Contact a bondsman (many are available 24/7)
2. Complete application and provide identification
3. Pay the fee (cash, credit card, or payment plan)

4. Bondsman posts bond with the court
5. You're released (usually within a few hours)

Advantages:

- Only need 10-15% of the total bond amount upfront
- Bondsmen are experienced with the jail system and can expedite release
- Some bondsmen offer payment plans
- You're not tying up large amounts of your own money

Disadvantages:

- The fee is non-refundable, even if charges are dropped
- You may need collateral for large bonds
- Bondsman can revoke the bond and have you arrested if you violate conditions
- Additional restrictions beyond court-ordered conditions

Typical Fees in Texas:

- 10-15% of bond amount is standard
- Some bondsmen charge additional fees for payment plans
- Collateral may be required for bonds over certain amounts

Property Bond: Using Real Estate

How it Works: You use real estate as collateral for the bond. The property value must typically be 1.5-2 times the bond amount.

Requirements:

- Clear title to the property
- Current appraisal or tax assessment
- Property must be in Texas
- All owners must consent

Advantages:

- No cash upfront
- No bondsman fees
- You keep control of your property

Disadvantages:

- Lengthy approval process (can take several days)
- Risk losing property if you miss court
- Property must have sufficient equity
- Complex paperwork and legal requirements

Best For: People with significant real estate equity but limited cash.

Personal Recognizance (PR Bond)

How it Works: You're released on your promise to appear in court, without having to pay money upfront.

Who Qualifies:

- Strong community ties
- Stable employment and residence
- No flight risk concerns

Advantages:

- No money required
- Immediate release once approved
- No bondsman involvement

Disadvantages:

- Not available for serious charges
- Strict conditions often apply
- May require pretrial supervision
- Limited availability

SIDEBAR: KEY TERMS

BAIL:

The amount of money set by the court to secure your release.

BOND:

The actual mechanism used to secure your release (cash, surety, property, or PR).

BONDSMAN:

A licensed professional who posts bond for a fee.

COLLATERAL:

Property or assets used to secure a bond.

FORFEITURE:

Losing your bond money for failing to appear in court.

REVOCATION:

Having your bond cancelled and being returned to jail.

PRETRIAL SUPERVISION:

Monitoring while on bond (drug testing, check-ins, etc.).

BOND CONDITIONS: WHAT YOU MUST FOLLOW

Getting out on bond isn't just about paying money - you'll have conditions you must follow strictly. Violating these conditions can land you back in jail and forfeit your bond.

Standard Conditions (Apply to Everyone)

Appear for All Court Dates:

- This is the most important condition
- Missing court results in automatic bond forfeiture
- Always confirm court dates with your attorney

No New Criminal Activity:

- Any arrest while on bond can revoke your release
- This includes minor offenses like traffic tickets in some cases
- Be extra careful about your behavior

Stay in Designated Geographic Area:

- Usually limited to certain counties
- Travel restrictions may apply
- Get permission before leaving the area

Keep Contact Information Current:

- Notify the court of address changes
- Maintain working phone number
- Inform your attorney of any changes

Common Additional Conditions for Drug Cases

No Drug or Alcohol Use:

- Zero tolerance policies are common
- Random drug testing required

- Failed tests can result in immediate jail time

Regular Check-Ins:

- Weekly or monthly meetings with pretrial services
- Phone check-ins may be required
- GPS monitoring in some cases

No Contact with Co-Defendants:

- Can't communicate with others charged in the same case
- Includes social media contact
- Family gatherings may be complicated if relatives are co-defendants

No Possession of Weapons:

- All firearms must be surrendered
- Includes legally owned weapons
- Even knife possession may be prohibited

Employment/Education Requirements:

- Maintain current job or actively seek employment
- Continue with school if enrolled
- May require verification from employers/schools

Special Conditions

Drug Treatment Programs:

- Enrollment in counseling or rehabilitation
- Regular attendance required
- Progress reports to the court

Community Service:

- Specific number of hours required
- Must be completed before trial
- Approved organizations only

No Driving:

- License surrender in some cases
- Especially common in cases involving vehicles
- May affect ability to work

⚠ **CRITICAL WARNING**

Bond conditions are not suggestions - they're court orders. Violating any condition can result in immediate arrest, bond revocation, and having to stay in jail until your case ends. When in doubt about whether something violates your conditions, ask your attorney first.

THE FINANCIAL REALITY: MAKING BOND WORK

Calculating True Costs

Bondsman Route ($5,000 bond example):

- 10% fee: $500 (non-refundable)
- Additional fees: $50-100
- Total cost: $550-600

Cash Bond Route ($5,000 bond example):

- Full amount: $5,000 (refundable minus small fees)
- Administrative fees: $25-50
- Total cost: $25-50 (if you appear for all court dates)

Payment Options for Bondsmen

Full Payment Upfront:

- Pay entire fee when posting bond
- No additional interest or fees
- Fastest release option

Payment Plans:

- Some bondsmen offer financing
- Higher total cost due to interest
- May require collateral
- Strict payment schedules

Collateral Options:

- Vehicle titles
- Real estate deeds
- Valuable personal property
- Co-signers with good credit

What They Can Do:

- Pay bondsman fees on your behalf
- Provide collateral for bonds
- Co-sign with bondsmen
- Post cash bonds using their money

What They're Risking:

- If you miss court, they lose their money/property
- They may be legally responsible for the full bond amount
- Bondsmen can pursue them for payment
- Their credit may be affected

BOND DECISION CHECKLIST

BEFORE CHOOSING YOUR BOND OPTION:

- ☐ How much cash do I have available immediately?
- ☐ Will I need money for attorney fees?
- ☐ How long might my case take to resolve?
- ☐ Do I have family/friends who can help?
- ☐ What are the total costs of each option?
- ☐ Can I comply with likely bond conditions?
- ☐ Do I have collateral if needed?

GETTING BOND REDUCED

If your bail amount is too high, you're not stuck with it. You can petition the court for a bond reduction.

Grounds for Bond Reduction

Changed Circumstances:

- New information about your ties to the community
- Employment verification
- Family responsibilities
- Medical needs

Financial Hardship:

- Inability to pay current amount
- Loss of income due to arrest
- Family financial responsibilities

Excessive Bail:

- Amount is disproportionate to the charges
- Comparison to similar cases
- Constitutional challenges

The Process

File a Motion: Your attorney submits a formal request to reduce bond.

Present Evidence: Gather documents showing:

- Employment history
- Community ties
- Financial situation
- Character references
- Family responsibilities

Court Hearing: A judge will consider the evidence and decide whether to reduce bail.

New Bond Amount: If successful, you can post the lower amount and be released.

COMMON BOND MISTAKES TO AVOID

Using Disreputable Bondsmen

Warning Signs:

- Requesting sexual favors or inappropriate collateral
- Demanding excessive fees (over 15%)
- No proper licensing
- High-pressure tactics
- Poor reviews or complaints

How to Choose a Good Bondsman:

- Check licensing with the state
- Read online reviews
- Ask for referrals from attorneys
- Compare fees and terms
- Make sure they're available 24/7

Violating Bond Conditions

Most Common Violations:

- Failed drug tests
- Missing check-in appointments
- Contact with prohibited persons
- Leaving authorized geographic area
- New arrests

Consequences:

- Immediate return to jail
- Bond forfeiture (lose your money)
- Higher bond on new charges
- More restrictive conditions if released again

Not Understanding the Financial Commitment

Remember:

- Bondsman fees are never refundable
- You're responsible for the full bond amount if you miss court
- Additional fees may apply throughout the process
- Your case ending doesn't automatically end your obligations

STRATEGIC TIP

If you're choosing between using a bondsman or depleting your savings for a cash bond, consider how much you'll need for attorney fees and other case expenses. Sometimes paying a bondsman fee preserves cash you'll need later for your defense.

LIFE ON BOND: WHAT TO EXPECT

Pretrial Supervision

Many people on bond must report to pretrial services, which may include:

Regular Check-Ins:

- In-person meetings weekly or monthly
- Phone check-ins between meetings
- GPS monitoring via ankle bracelet

Drug Testing:

- Random urine tests
- Breathalyzer tests for alcohol
- Hair follicle tests for longer detection periods

Reporting Requirements:

- Employment verification
- Address confirmation
- Court date reminders

Managing Bond Conditions

Create a System:

- Calendar all check-in dates
- Set reminders for court dates
- Keep contact information current
- Document compliance

Stay in Communication:

- Regular contact with your attorney
- Notify pretrial services of any issues
- Ask questions when unsure about conditions

Plan for Success:

- Arrange reliable transportation to check-ins
- Build support systems
- Address underlying issues (like substance abuse)

FREQUENTLY ASKED QUESTIONS

Q **What happens if I can't afford bond at all?**

A You can request a hearing to argue for bond reduction or release on personal recognizance. Some jurisdictions have pretrial services programs to help indigent defendants.

Q **Can bond be denied completely?**

A In Texas, most people have a right to reasonable bail. Bond can only be denied in capital murder cases or when specific legal standards are met.

Q **What if my bondsman wants to revoke my bond?**

A Bondsmen can surrender your bond and have you arrested, but they must follow proper procedures. Contact your attorney immediately if this happens.

Q **Can I switch bondsmen?**

A Generally no, unless the current bondsman agrees to surrender the bond. You'd need to pay a new bondsman and meet their requirements.

Q **What happens to my bond money when my case ends?**

A Cash bonds are refunded minus administrative fees. Bondsman fees are never refunded, regardless of your case outcome.

WHAT NANCY DECIDED

"After talking with my attorney and looking at my finances, I decided to use a bondsman. Yes, I lost the $500 fee, but I kept my savings available for attorney fees and living expenses during the case. It was the right decision for my situation, even though it cost more in the long run."

Moving Forward: Your Path Home

Getting out on bond is about more than just money - it's about maintaining your life, your job, and your family relationships while you fight your case. You now understand:

- How bail amounts are set and what factors influence them
- The different types of bonds available and their costs
- What conditions you'll need to follow to stay out of jail
- How to avoid common mistakes that could land you back in custody
- When and how to seek bond reduction

Remember, being released on bond is a privilege, not a right. Use this opportunity wisely to work with your attorney, address any underlying issues, and show the court that you're taking your situation seriously.

In the next chapter, we'll help you find and work effectively with a criminal defense attorney - one of the most important decisions you'll make in your case.

CHAPTER 5:

FINDING AND WORKING WITH A CRIMINAL DEFENSE ATTORNEY

Nancy sat in her car outside the first law office, too nervous to go inside. She'd never needed a criminal defense attorney before and had no idea what to expect. Would they judge her? Could she even afford a good lawyer? The whole situation felt overwhelming - here she was, a healthcare professional who helped people for a living, now needing help herself in a world she didn't understand.

If you're feeling lost about finding an attorney, you're not alone. Most people have never had to hire a criminal defense lawyer, and the process can feel intimidating when you're already dealing with so much stress. You might be worried about the cost, concerned about finding someone who actually cares about your case, or simply unsure what questions to ask. These feelings are completely normal.

The truth is, there are many skilled attorneys in Texas who understand that good people sometimes find themselves in difficult situations. They've seen cases like yours before, and they know that a drug charge doesn't define who you are as a person. Finding the right lawyer isn't about finding someone to perform miracles - it's about finding someone who will listen to your story, explain your options clearly, and fight hard for the best possible outcome. This chapter will help you navigate that search with confidence and find an attorney who's the right fit for you and your situation.

📖 IF YOU ONLY READ ONE THING IN THIS CHAPTER

Start calling attorneys TODAY for a consultation. Ask three questions:

(1) How many drug cases do you handle?

(2) What do you think about my situation?

(3) What are your fees and payment options?

Don't overthink it - just start making calls.

ATTORNEY SEARCH CHECKLIST

Before You Start Looking:

- [ ] Determine your budget for legal fees
- [ ] Gather basic information about your charges
- [ ] List your main concerns and goals
- [ ] Ask friends/family for referrals
- [ ] Research your local bar association

During Initial Consultations:

- [ ] Ask about their experience with drug cases
- [ ] Discuss fee structure and payment options
- [ ] Evaluate their communication style
- [ ] Ask about their strategy for your case
- [ ] Get a feel for their availability and responsiveness

WHY YOU NEED A CRIMINAL DEFENSE ATTORNEY

Some people think they can handle drug charges on their own, especially if they're "just" facing possession charges. This is almost always a mistake. Here's why professional legal representation is crucial:

The Legal System is Complex

Criminal law involves intricate procedures, deadlines, and rules that aren't obvious to non-lawyers. Missing a filing deadline or failing to make the right objection at trial can destroy your case permanently.

Nancy's Reality Check: «I thought my case was simple - I had pills without a prescription. But my attorney found problems with the search, issues with the lab testing, and opportunities for pretrial diversion that I never would have known existed.»

Prosecutors Have Extensive Resources

The state has experienced prosecutors, investigators, and crime labs working to convict you. Facing this alone puts you at a severe disadvantage.

The Stakes are Too High

Drug convictions can affect your employment, professional licenses, immigration status, and housing opportunities for years to come. This isn't the time to try to save money by representing yourself.

Attorneys See Options You Don't

Experienced criminal defense lawyers know about:

- Pretrial diversion programs
- Plea bargain opportunities
- Procedural defenses
- Sentencing alternatives
- Appeal possibilities

UNDERSTANDING THE INVESTMENT

Hiring an attorney isn't just an expense - it's an investment in your future. The cost of good legal representation is almost always less than the long-term consequences of a conviction on your employment, professional licenses, and other opportunities.

TYPES OF CRIMINAL DEFENSE ATTORNEYS

Not all attorneys are the same, and understanding the differences helps you make a better choice.

Solo Practitioners

Advantages:

- Direct access to the attorney handling your case
- Often more affordable than large firms
- Personalized attention
- Flexible with payment arrangements

Potential Drawbacks:

- Limited resources for complex cases
- May have heavy caseloads
- Less backup if attorney becomes unavailable

Best For: Straightforward cases, clients who want direct attorney contact, budget-conscious clients.

Small Criminal Defense Firms (2-5 attorneys)

Advantages:

- Specialized focus on criminal law
- More resources than solo practitioners
- Attorney backup and coverage
- Reasonable fees

Potential Drawbacks:

- May not handle the most complex cases
- Limited support staff

Best For: Most drug cases, clients who want specialized expertise with personal attention.

Large Criminal Defense Firms

Advantages:

- Extensive resources and support staff
- Multiple attorneys with different specialties
- Experience with complex cases
- Investigative capabilities

Potential Drawbacks:

- Higher fees
- Less personal attention
- May assign case to junior attorneys

Best For: Complex cases, clients facing serious charges, those with significant assets at risk.

SIDEBAR: KEY TERMS

RETAINER:

Upfront payment to secure an attorney's services.

FLAT FEE:

Fixed price for handling your entire case.

HOURLY RATE:

Payment based on time spent on your case.

CONTINGENCY FEE:

Payment only if case is successful (rare in criminal cases).

CONFLICT OF INTEREST:

Situation where attorney cannot represent you due to competing loyalties.

ATTORNEY-CLIENT PRIVILEGE:

Legal protection that keeps your conversations with your lawyer confidential.

DISCOVERY:

Process of obtaining evidence from the prosecution.

FINDING ATTORNEY CANDIDATES

Getting Referrals

State Bar Association: The Texas State Bar has a lawyer referral service that can connect you with criminal defense attorneys in your area.

Local Bar Associations: County bar associations often have specialized referral services for criminal cases.

Other Attorneys: If you know any lawyers (even in other areas of law), they can often provide excellent referrals to criminal defense specialists.

Personal Referrals: Friends, family, or coworkers who have used criminal defense attorneys can provide valuable insights.

Online Resources:

- State bar websites
- Legal directories like Avvo or Martindale-Hubbell
- Attorney websites and reviews
- Court records to see who handles cases like yours

Researching Potential Attorneys

Check Their Background:

- Years of experience in criminal law
- Specific experience with drug cases
- Education and training
- Bar disciplinary history
- Professional associations and memberships

Look at Their Track Record:

- Types of cases they handle
- Results they've achieved
- Client testimonials
- Peer recognition

Evaluate Their Resources:

- Office location and facilities
- Support staff
- Technology and case management systems
- Relationships with experts and investigators

THE INITIAL CONSULTATION

Most criminal defense attorneys offer free initial consultations. Use this time wisely to evaluate both the attorney and your case.

What to Bring

Essential Documents:

- Arrest report or citation
- Bond paperwork
- Court notices
- Police reports (if available)
- Any correspondence from prosecutors

Personal Information:

- Employment history
- Criminal history (be honest)
- Financial information for fee discussion
- List of questions and concerns

Questions to Ask

About Their Experience:

- How many drug cases do you handle per year?
- What's your experience with cases like mine?
- How familiar are you with the prosecutors and judges in my jurisdiction?
- What's your success rate with similar cases?

About Your Case:

- What are the strengths and weaknesses of my case?
- What's your initial strategy?
- What are my realistic options?
- What's the likely timeline for resolution?

About Fees and Costs:

- What's your fee structure?
- What's included in your fee?
- Are there additional costs I should expect?
- Do you offer payment plans?

About Communication:

- How often will you update me on my case?
- How quickly do you return phone calls?
- Who else in your office might work on my case?
- How do you prefer to communicate (phone, email, in-person)?

⚠️ RED FLAGS TO AVOID

Run away from attorneys who:

- Guarantee specific outcomes
- Ask for payment in cash only
- Seem unfamiliar with local courts and procedures
- Don't return calls promptly during the consultation process
- Have multiple bar complaints or disciplinary actions

UNDERSTANDING LEGAL FEES

Legal fees are often the biggest concern when hiring an attorney. Understanding fee structures helps you budget and avoid surprises.

Common Fee Structures

Flat Fee (Most Common for Drug Cases):

- One price covers your entire case through trial
- Usually includes arraignment, pretrial motions, plea negotiations, and trial
- May not include appeals
- Allows you to budget accurately

Hourly Rate:

- Pay for time actually spent on your case
- Rates typically range from $300-800+ per hour
- Can be unpredictable for budgeting
- More common for complex cases

Retainer Plus Hourly:

- Pay a retainer upfront, then hourly charges against it
- Allows attorney to start work immediately
- May require additional payments as case progresses

What's Typically Included

Standard Services:

- Initial case review and strategy development
- Arraignment and early court appearances
- Discovery review and analysis
- Pretrial motion practice
- Plea negotiations
- Trial preparation and representation

Additional Costs:

- Appeals (usually separate fee)
- Expert witnesses
- Investigators
- Court reporters for depositions
- Travel expenses for out-of-town cases

Payment Options

Full Payment Upfront:

- Often results in lower total fees
- Ensures attorney is fully paid
- May strain your finances

Payment Plans:

- Spread costs over several months
- Usually requires some money upfront
- May include interest or financing fees

Family Assistance:

- Having family pay attorney fees
- Can preserve your income for living expenses
- Make sure everyone understands the arrangement

WORKING EFFECTIVELY WITH YOUR ATTORNEY

Once you've hired an attorney, the quality of your working relationship significantly affects your case outcome.

Your Responsibilities as a Client

Be Completely Honest: Your attorney needs all the facts to develop the best strategy. Lying or omitting important information can destroy your case.

Follow Instructions: If your attorney tells you to do something (or not do something), follow those instructions exactly.

Communicate Promptly: Return calls quickly and keep your attorney informed of any developments in your case or life.

Prepare for Meetings: Come to meetings with questions prepared and necessary documents organized.

Pay Bills on Time: Nothing derails a case faster than fee disputes. Communicate with your attorney if you're having payment problems.

What to Expect from Your Attorney

Regular Communication: Your attorney should keep you informed about important developments and return calls within a reasonable time.

Honest Assessment: A good attorney will give you realistic expectations about your case, not false hope.

Thorough Preparation: Your attorney should review all evidence, research legal issues, and prepare thoroughly for court appearances.

Professional Representation: Your attorney should present your case professionally in court and in negotiations.

Zealous Advocacy: Your attorney should fight hard for the best possible outcome while working within ethical bounds.

ATTORNEY EVALUATION SCORECARD

Rate each attorney you consult (1-5 scale):

Experience & Expertise:

- ☐ Years practicing criminal law
- ☐ Specific drug case experience
- ☐ Knowledge of local courts
- ☐ Professional credentials

Communication:

- ☐ Returns calls promptly
- ☐ Explains things clearly
- ☐ Listens to your concerns
- ☐ Makes you feel comfortable

Strategy & Approach:

- ☐ Realistic about your case
- ☐ Explains potential strategies
- ☐ Discusses all options
- ☐ Shows genuine interest

Fees & Value:

- ☐ Reasonable fee structure
- ☐ Clear about costs
- ☐ Offers payment options
- ☐ Good value for services

SPECIAL CONSIDERATIONS FOR DRUG CASES

Drug cases have unique aspects that require specific expertise and experience.

Scientific Evidence

Drug cases often involve:

- Lab testing and chain of custody issues
- Expert testimony about substances
- Technical challenges to evidence
- Understanding of testing procedures

What This Means: Look for attorneys who have successfully challenged lab evidence in drug cases.

Diversion and Treatment Programs

Many drug cases can be resolved through:

- Pretrial diversion programs
- Drug court participation
- Treatment-based plea agreements
- Community service alternatives

What This Means: Your attorney should be familiar with all available programs in your jurisdiction.

Collateral Consequences

Drug convictions can affect:

- Professional licenses
- Immigration status
- Employment opportunities
- Educational financial aid

What This Means: Your attorney should understand and discuss these broader implications.

WHEN THINGS GO WRONG

Sometimes the attorney-client relationship doesn't work out. Here's how to handle problems:

Communication Issues

Try Direct Communication First:

- Schedule a meeting to discuss your concerns
- Be specific about what's bothering you
- Give your attorney a chance to improve

Document Problems:

- Keep records of missed calls or meetings
- Save emails and correspondence
- Note important deadlines that are missed

Performance Problems

Serious Issues:

- Missing court dates
- Failing to file important motions
- Not returning calls for weeks
- Appearing unprepared in court

What You Can Do:

- File a complaint with the state bar
- Seek a second opinion from another attorney
- Consider changing attorneys (with court permission)

Changing Attorneys

When It Might Be Necessary:

- Complete breakdown in communication
- Attorney appears incompetent
- Serious ethical violations
- Conflict of interest develops

How to Do It:

- Find new attorney first
- File motion to substitute counsel
- Resolve fee issues with old attorney
- Ensure smooth transition of case files

💡 NANCY'S LESSON

"I interviewed three attorneys before choosing one. The first was too expensive, the second seemed rushed and uninterested, but the third took time to understand my situation and explained everything clearly. That extra effort in choosing the right attorney made all the difference in my case outcome."

FREQUENTLY ASKED QUESTIONS

Q **How much should I expect to pay for a drug case attorney?**

A Fees vary widely based on location, case complexity, and attorney experience. Simple possession cases might cost $3,500-$7,500, while more complex cases can cost much more.

Q **Should I hire the most expensive attorney I can afford?**

A Not necessarily. Look for the best combination of experience, communication, and value. The most expensive attorney isn't always the best for your specific case.

Q **Can I change attorneys in the middle of my case?**

A Yes, but it requires court approval and can delay your case. Try to resolve issues with your current attorney first.

Q **What if I can't afford any attorney?**

A You may qualify for court-appointed counsel. Apply at your arraignment or contact the court clerk's office.

Q **Should I hire an attorney even if I plan to plead guilty?**

A Absolutely. An attorney can help negotiate better plea terms, explore alternatives to conviction, and protect your rights during sentencing.

BUILDING THE RIGHT ATTORNEY-CLIENT RELATIONSHIP

The attorney you choose will be your guide through one of the most stressful experiences of your life. Take time to find someone who:

- Has the experience and expertise to handle your case effectively
- Communicates in a way that makes sense to you
- Treats you with respect and understanding
- Offers fair and transparent fee arrangements
- Makes you feel confident about your representation

Remember, you're not just hiring a lawyer - you're hiring an advocate, counselor, and strategic partner for your case. The right attorney can make the difference between a conviction that follows you for life and a resolution that allows you to move forward with minimal long-term consequences.

Your future is worth the investment in quality legal representation. Take the time to find the right attorney, and then work with them as a team to achieve the best possible outcome for your situation.

In the next chapter, we'll explore the pretrial phase of your case - the critical period when your attorney gathers evidence, files motions, and builds your defense strategy.

CHAPTER 6:

PRETRIAL MOTIONS

AND DISCOVERY

After Nancy hired her attorney, she expected things to move quickly toward some kind of resolution. Instead, weeks went by with what seemed like nothing happening. Her lawyer mentioned filing "motions" and waiting for "discovery," but Nancy had no clue what any of that meant. Was her attorney actually working on her case, or just collecting fees while her life hung in limbo?

Here's what's really going on during those seemingly quiet weeks: your attorney is doing some of the most important work of your entire case. Think of this phase like preparing for a big exam - you can't just show up and wing it. Your lawyer needs to see all the evidence against you, figure out if the police followed proper procedures, and identify any weaknesses in the state's case. It's detective work, really, and it can make or break your outcome.

I know it's frustrating when you just want this whole thing to be over, but this behind-the-scenes work is where cases are often won or lost. Your attorney might discover that the search was illegal, the evidence was mishandled, or the police reports contain contradictions. Sometimes these discoveries can get your charges reduced or even dismissed entirely. This chapter will walk you through what's happening during this crucial phase, so you understand why patience now can pay off big time later.

PRETRIAL PHASE TIMELINE

Week 1-2 After Hiring Attorney:

- ☐ Attorney requests discovery from prosecution
- ☐ Initial case file review begins
- ☐ Client interview and fact gathering
- ☐ Preliminary legal research

Week 3-6:

- ☐ Discovery materials received and analyzed
- ☐ Investigation of potential defenses
- ☐ Witness interviews if necessary
- ☐ Expert consultation if needed

Week 6-12:

- ☐ Pretrial motions filed if appropriate
- ☐ Motion hearings scheduled and conducted
- ☐ Plea negotiations may begin
- ☐ Trial preparation starts if no plea agreement

WHAT IS DISCOVERY?

Discovery is the legal process that allows your attorney to obtain evidence from the prosecution. It's like getting to see the other team's playbook before the game starts.

The Michael Morton Act: Your Right to See the Evidence

In Texas, the Michael Morton Act significantly expanded defendants' rights to discovery. Named after a man who was wrongfully convicted due to prosecutors withholding evidence, this law requires the state to provide much more information than before.

What the Michael Morton Act Requires:

- Prosecutors must disclose all evidence, not just what they plan to use at trial
- This includes evidence that might help your defense
- Police reports, witness statements, and investigative materials must be shared
- The disclosure must happen early in the case, not right before trial

Why This Matters for Your Case: Your attorney can now see the complete picture of the state's investigation, including evidence that might help prove your innocence or reduce your charges.

What Your Attorney Will Receive

Police Reports:

- Arresting officer's report
- Witness statements
- Investigative reports
- Supplemental reports from follow-up investigation

Physical Evidence:

- Lab reports on suspected drugs
- Photos of evidence
- Chain of custody documents
- Evidence logs and inventories

Witness Information:

- Names and contact information for prosecution witnesses
- Statements given by witnesses
- Expert witness reports
- Character evidence about witnesses

Audio and Video:

- Dash cam footage from police vehicles
- Body camera recordings
- Jail phone recordings
- Surveillance footage from the scene

Digital Evidence:

- Text messages from your phone
- Social media posts
- GPS data
- Call logs and records

NANCY'S DISCOVERY SURPRISE

"My attorney found inconsistencies in the police reports that I never would have noticed. The arresting officer said he smelled marijuana in his report, but I was arrested for prescription pills, not marijuana. Little details like that can be important for challenging the search."

CRITICAL EVIDENCE ANALYSIS

Your attorney will carefully examine every piece of evidence looking for problems, inconsistencies, and opportunities to challenge the state's case.

Lab Reports and Chain of Custody

What Your Attorney Looks For:

- Proper collection procedures
- Unbroken chain of custody
- Correct testing methods
- Equipment calibration records
- Lab technician qualifications

Common Problems:

- Evidence stored improperly
- Gaps in the chain of custody
- Lab technician errors
- Equipment malfunctions
- Contamination issues

Real Example: Maria's case was dismissed when her attorney discovered that the evidence room had a temperature control failure, potentially affecting the integrity of the drug samples.

Search and Seizure Issues

Fourth Amendment Requirements:

- Valid reason for the initial stop
- Proper consent or warrant for searches
- Scope of search within legal limits
- No coercion in obtaining consent

Common Constitutional Violations:

- Unlawful traffic stops
- Searches without consent or warrants
- Exceeding the scope of consent
- Coercive questioning

Police Report Inconsistencies

What Your Attorney Compares:

- Different officers' versions of events
- Officer testimony vs. written reports
- Physical evidence vs. described evidence
- Timeline inconsistencies

Red Flags:

- Reports written days after the incident
- Identical language in multiple officers' reports
- Details that don't match physical evidence
- Missing information about key events

SIDEBAR: KEY TERMS

DISCOVERY:

The legal process of obtaining evidence from the prosecution.

MOTION TO SUPPRESS:

Request to exclude illegally obtained evidence.

CHAIN OF CUSTODY:

Documentation showing who handled evidence and when.

BRADY MATERIAL:

Evidence favorable to the defense that the prosecution must disclose.

EXCULPATORY EVIDENCE:

Evidence that tends to prove innocence or reduce culpability.

SIDEBAR: KEY TERMS

FOURTH AMENDMENT:

Constitutional protection against unreasonable searches and seizures.

PROBABLE CAUSE:

Standard of evidence needed to justify an arrest or search warrant.

MICHAEL MORTON ACT:

Texas law that says prosecutors must share ALL evidence with your attorney, not just the evidence they plan to use against you. This gives your lawyer a complete picture of what the state knows.

TYPES OF PRETRIAL MOTIONS

Pretrial motions are formal requests to the court asking for specific rulings before trial. Think of them as your attorney's way of fighting for your rights and challenging improper evidence.

Motion to Suppress Evidence

Purpose: Exclude evidence obtained in violation of your constitutional rights.

Common Grounds:

- Illegal search and seizure
- Statements made without Miranda warnings
- Evidence obtained through illegal stops
- Coerced confessions

Process:

- Attorney files written motion with legal arguments
- Court schedules suppression hearing
- Police officers testify about their actions
- Your attorney cross-examines officers
- Judge rules on whether evidence can be used

Potential Outcomes:

- Evidence suppressed (excluded from trial)
- Motion denied (evidence can be used)
- Partial suppression (some evidence excluded)

Motion to Dismiss

Purpose: Ask the court to dismiss charges entirely.

Common Grounds:

- Insufficient evidence
- Procedural violations
- Statute of limitations expired
- Double jeopardy issues

Reality Check: Motions to dismiss are rarely granted in drug cases unless there are serious procedural problems.

Motion for Speedy Trial

Purpose: Force the prosecution to try your case within legal time limits.

When It's Used:

- Case has been delayed for extended periods
- Prosecution isn't ready for trial
- Witnesses become unavailable due to delays

Discovery Motions

Purpose: Compel the prosecution to provide additional evidence.

Common Requests:

- Police personnel files
- Lab equipment maintenance records
- Training records for officers
- Policies and procedures manuals

THE SUPPRESSION HEARING: YOUR DAY IN COURT

If your attorney files a motion to suppress, you'll have a hearing where the judge decides whether the evidence against you was legally obtained.

How Suppression Hearings Work

The State's Case:

- Prosecutors call police officers to testify
- Officers describe what they did and why
- State tries to justify the search or seizure

Your Defense:

- Your attorney cross-examines the officers
- May call witnesses on your behalf
- Argues that officers violated your rights

The Judge's Decision:

- Reviews the law and facts presented
- Determines if constitutional violations occurred
- Rules on what evidence can be used at trial

What Makes a Strong Suppression Motion

Clear Constitutional Violations:

- Searches without warrants, consent, or legal justification
- Arrests without probable cause
- Statements taken in violation of Miranda rights

Good Documentation:

- Video or audio recordings of the incident
- Written policies that were violated
- Expert testimony about proper procedures

Credible Witnesses:

- Independent witnesses to the incident
- Your testimony (in some circumstances)
- Expert witnesses about police procedures

⚠️ **SUPPRESSION HEARING REALITY**

Judges often defer to police officers' testimony, especially when there's no video evidence. Winning suppression motions requires clear evidence of constitutional violations, not just claims that officers acted improperly.

BUILDING YOUR DEFENSE STRATEGY

During the pretrial phase, your attorney develops the overall strategy for your case based on the evidence and legal issues discovered.

Possible Defense Strategies

Challenge the Evidence:

- Question lab results and testing procedures
- Challenge chain of custody
- Dispute the reliability of field tests

Constitutional Defenses:

- Illegal search and seizure
- Lack of probable cause for arrest
- Miranda violations

Factual Defenses:

- Lack of knowledge about the drugs
- Constructive possession challenges
- Innocent explanation for the evidence

Procedural Defenses:

- Statute of limitations
- Speedy trial violations
- Discovery violations

Case Investigation

Witness Interviews: Your attorney may interview potential witnesses to:

- Corroborate your version of events
- Identify problems with the state's case
- Gather character evidence for sentencing

Expert Consultation: Depending on your case, your attorney might consult:

- Forensic experts to challenge lab results
- Former police officers to critique procedures
- Medical experts for prescription drug cases

Scene Investigation: Your attorney may visit the location where you were arrested to:

- Understand the physical layout
- Take photographs
- Identify potential witnesses

CLIENT COOPERATION CHECKLIST

How You Can Help During Pretrial Phase:

Provide Complete Information:

- ☐ Tell your attorney everything about the incident
- ☐ Identify potential witnesses
- ☐ Provide character references
- ☐ Share any medical or prescription records

Gather Helpful Documents:

- ☐ Employment records
- ☐ Medical records
- ☐ Prescription histories
- ☐ Character references
- ☐ Financial records (for sentencing)

Stay Available:

- ☐ Return attorney calls promptly
- ☐ Keep contact information current
- ☐ Be available for meetings and hearings
- ☐ Follow all bond conditions

COMMON PRETRIAL DISCOVERIES

Understanding what attorneys commonly find during pretrial investigation helps you appreciate why this phase is so important.

Police Procedure Violations

Miranda Issues:

- Questioning without proper warnings
- Continuing interrogation after requesting a lawyer
- Using statements obtained in violation of Miranda

Search Problems:

- Consent obtained through coercion
- Searches exceeding the scope of consent
- Vehicle searches without proper justification

Evidence Handling Problems

Chain of Custody Gaps:

- Missing documentation
- Unauthorized access to evidence
- Improper storage conditions

Lab Issues:

- Equipment not properly calibrated
- Contaminated samples
- Unqualified technicians

Report Inconsistencies

Officer Contradictions:

- Different versions of the same events
- Timeline problems
- Physical evidence inconsistent with reports

Witness Statement Problems:

- Coached or leading questions
- Statements that contradict physical evidence
- Reliability issues with witnesses

PLEA NEGOTIATIONS BEGIN

Often during the pretrial phase, prosecutors will make initial plea offers based on their assessment of the case's strengths and weaknesses.

How Discovery Affects Plea Offers

Strong State Case:

- Few constitutional issues
- Solid evidence
- Credible witnesses
- Limited plea concessions

Weak State Case:

- Evidence problems discovered
- Constitutional violations likely
- Witness credibility issues
- Better plea offers possible

Timing of Negotiations

Early Offers:

- Often less favorable
- Before defense investigation complete
- Based on police reports only

Post-Discovery Offers:

- More realistic assessments
- Account for evidence problems
- Reflect true case strength

💡 **STRATEGIC PATIENCE**

Don't pressure your attorney to accept early plea offers. The best deals often come after thorough investigation reveals problems with the state's case. Patience during the pretrial phase can result in significantly better outcomes.

WHEN PRETRIAL MOTIONS WIN CASES

Sometimes pretrial motions don't just improve your position - they end your case entirely.

Cases Dismissed Due to Suppression

Illegal Stops:

- Traffic stops without reasonable suspicion
- Pretextual stops for minor violations
- Stops based on racial profiling

Illegal Searches:

- Searches without consent or warrants
- Searches exceeding the scope of consent
- Searches based on false information

Cases Dismissed Due to Discovery Violations

Michael Morton Act Violations:

- Prosecution fails to disclose required evidence
- Late disclosure that prejudices the defense
- Withholding evidence that could help the defendant

Brady Violations:

- Prosecution fails to disclose exculpatory evidence
- Late disclosure of important evidence
- Destruction of potentially helpful evidence

Speedy Trial Violations:

- Excessive delays in prosecution
- State not ready for trial within time limits
- Prejudice to defendant from delays

FREQUENTLY ASKED QUESTIONS

Q **How long does the pretrial phase usually last?**

A Typically 3-6 months for most drug cases, but complex cases can take longer. Serious cases with multiple motions might take a year or more.

Q **Will I have to testify at pretrial hearings?**

A Usually not. Most pretrial motions involve legal arguments and police testimony. Your attorney will advise if your testimony would be helpful.

Q **What happens if we win a motion to suppress?**

A If key evidence is suppressed, the prosecution may dismiss charges or offer a much better plea deal. Sometimes suppression wins the entire case.

Q **Should I be worried if my attorney isn't filing motions?**

A Not necessarily. Motion practice depends on the specific facts of your case. If there are no constitutional violations, filing motions might be counterproductive.

Q **Can new evidence be discovered after the pretrial phase?**

A Yes, but there are deadlines for disclosure. Late-discovered evidence might not be admissible unless there's a good reason for the delay.

WHAT NANCY LEARNED

"I was so impatient during the pretrial phase because I just wanted everything resolved. But my attorney's careful review of the evidence found problems with how the search was conducted. Those problems didn't get my case dismissed, but they definitely helped in plea negotiations. I got a much better deal than I would have if we'd rushed into a plea agreement."

The Value of Thorough Preparation

The pretrial phase might seem slow and frustrating, but it's where your defense is built. During this time, your attorney is:

- Examining every piece of evidence for weaknesses
- Identifying constitutional violations that could exclude evidence
- Building relationships and credibility with prosecutors
- Developing the strongest possible defense strategy
- Positioning your case for the best possible outcome

Trust the process and support your attorney's thorough preparation. The work done during the pretrial phase often determines whether you go to trial, accept a plea agreement, or even have your case dismissed entirely.

In the next chapter, we'll explore pretrial diversion programs - opportunities for second chances that can help you avoid a conviction altogether.

CHAPTER 7:

PRETRIAL DIVERSION PROGRAMS - SECOND CHANCES

When Nancy's attorney first mentioned pretrial diversion, she could hardly believe what she was hearing. "You mean there's a way to avoid a conviction entirely?" she asked. After weeks of worrying about losing her nursing license and having a permanent criminal record, the possibility of a fresh start seemed too good to be true. But her attorney explained that Texas recognizes something important: good people sometimes make mistakes, and the justice system doesn't have to destroy lives to achieve justice.

This is your chapter of hope. If you've been beating yourself up about your arrest, wondering how you'll ever recover from this mistake, I want you to take a deep breath and realize something: your story doesn't have to end with a conviction. Pretrial diversion programs exist because lawmakers understand that addiction is a health issue, not just a criminal one, and that people like you deserve a chance to prove they can turn things around.

You're not just a case number or a statistic - you're someone with a future worth fighting for. Whether you're a parent who needs to be there for your kids, a professional who worked hard to build a career, or simply someone who made a mistake and wants to do better, diversion programs can be your pathway back to the life you want. This chapter will show you how these programs work, who qualifies, and most importantly, how you can position yourself as the ideal candidate for a second chance. Your mistake doesn't define you, but what you do next absolutely can.

DIVERSION PROGRAM QUICK GUIDE

What Pretrial Diversion Offers:

- ☐ Charges dismissed upon successful completion
- ☐ No conviction on your record
- ☐ Opportunity to address underlying issues
- ☐ Maintain employment and professional licenses
- ☐ Avoid jail time and lengthy probation

Common Requirements:

- ☐ Admit responsibility for your actions
- ☐ Complete drug education or treatment
- ☐ Perform community service hours
- ☐ Submit to regular drug testing
- ☐ Pay program fees and court costs

UNDERSTANDING PRETRIAL DIVERSION

Pretrial diversion is exactly what it sounds like - diverting your case away from the traditional criminal justice process before you go to trial or enter a plea.

How Diversion Works

Instead of This Traditional Path: Arrest → Charges → Plea/Trial → Conviction → Sentencing → Probation

You Get This Alternative Path: Arrest → Charges → Diversion Application → Program Completion → Charges Dismissed

The Key Difference: Upon successful completion of the diversion program, your charges are dismissed entirely. You don't have a conviction on your record, and in most cases, you can truthfully say you've never been convicted of a crime.

Who Makes the Decision

Prosecutor's Discretion: In most Texas counties, the decision to offer diversion rests entirely with the prosecutor's office. They evaluate applications based on their own criteria and policies.

Defense Attorney's Role: Your attorney can advocate for your acceptance, provide supporting documentation, and present your case in the best possible light.

Judge's Involvement: Some counties require judicial approval, but typically the prosecutor's recommendation carries significant weight.

💡 **THE FRESH START OPPORTUNITY**

Diversion isn't just about avoiding conviction - it's about getting the help you need while preserving your future. Many people discover that the skills and insights they gain during diversion programs benefit them long after the legal case is closed.

TYPES OF DIVERSION PROGRAMS IN TEXAS

Different counties offer different programs, but most fall into these categories:

First Offender Programs

Who Qualifies:

- First-time drug offenders
- Non-violent charges only
- Usually limited to possession cases

Typical Requirements:

- Drug education classes
- Community service (20-80 hours)
- Regular check-ins with program coordinator
- Clean drug tests throughout the program
- Payment of fees ($300-800 typically)

Duration: Usually 6-12 months

Nancy's Path: Unfortunately Nancy did not qualify for a diversion program, which required 40 hours of community service, monthly drug tests, and completion of a drug education course. The decision was based on the prosecutor's discretion, and they did not recommend Nancy for a diversion program.

Treatment-Based Diversion

Who Qualifies:

- Offenders with documented substance abuse issues
- Willing to undergo assessment and treatment
- Usually requires admission of addiction problems

Typical Requirements:

- Comprehensive substance abuse evaluation

- Completion of recommended treatment (outpatient or inpatient)
- Regular counseling sessions
- Intensive drug testing
- Support group participation

Duration: 12-18 months typically

Veterans' Court Diversion

Who Qualifies:

- Military veterans with service-connected issues
- Often addresses PTSD, TBI, or substance abuse
- Requires military service verification

Typical Requirements:

- Mental health evaluation
- Treatment for underlying conditions
- Mentorship with other veterans
- Regular court appearances
- Compliance with treatment recommendations

Special Benefits: Designed specifically for veterans' unique needs and challenges.

Mental Health Diversion

Who Qualifies:

- Defendants with diagnosed mental health conditions
- Cases where mental illness contributed to the offense
- Willingness to undergo treatment

Typical Requirements:

- Psychiatric evaluation
- Medication compliance
- Regular therapy sessions
- Case management services
- Court monitoring

SIDEBAR: KEY TERMS

PRETRIAL DIVERSION:

Program allowing charges to be dismissed upon completion of requirements without a conviction.

DEFERRED PROSECUTION:

Formal agreement to postpone prosecution while defendant completes program requirements.

CONDITIONAL DISMISSAL:

Charges dismissed only if program requirements are successfully completed.

PROGRAM COORDINATOR:

Person who monitors compliance and reports progress to the court.

RESTITUTION:

Payment to victims for damages caused by the offense.

COMMUNITY SERVICE:

Unpaid work performed for nonprofit organizations or government agencies.

RECIDIVISM:

The tendency to re-offend after completing a program or sentence.

QUALIFYING FOR DIVERSION PROGRAMS

Not everyone is eligible for diversion, and criteria vary by county. Understanding what prosecutors look for helps you present the strongest possible application.

Common Eligibility Requirements

Criminal History:

- First-time offenders have the best chance
- Some programs accept people with very minor prior offenses
- Serious prior convictions usually disqualify applicants
- Recent arrests (even without convictions) may hurt your chances

Nature of the Current Offense:

- Simple possession charges are most likely to qualify
- Delivery or manufacturing charges rarely qualify
- Amount of drugs involved matters
- Presence of weapons usually disqualifies

Personal Circumstances:

- Stable employment or school enrollment
- Strong family support
- Community ties and involvement
- No flight risk concerns

Attitude and Motivation:

- Willingness to accept responsibility
- Genuine desire to address underlying issues
- Commitment to completing program requirements
- Understanding of the opportunity being offered

What Strengthens Your Application

Employment and Education:

- Steady work history
- Current employment
- Educational achievements
- Professional licenses at risk

Family Responsibilities:

- Dependent children
- Caregiving responsibilities
- Stable family relationships
- Community involvement

Character References:

- Letters from employers
- Community leaders' endorsements
- Religious leaders' support
- Family statements

Demonstration of Change:

- Voluntary enrollment in treatment
- Community service already performed
- Positive life changes since arrest
- Evidence of remorse and responsibility

THE APPLICATION PROCESS

Applying for diversion requires careful preparation and strategic presentation of your case.

Gathering Required Documents

Personal Information:

- Detailed personal history
- Employment records
- Educational transcripts
- Financial information

Character Evidence:

- Reference letters
- Community involvement documentation
- Awards or recognitions
- Professional achievements

Case-Specific Information:

- Detailed account of the offense
- Explanation of circumstances
- Evidence of remorse
- Plans for addressing underlying issues

Key Elements to Include:

- Accept responsibility for your actions
- Explain the circumstances without making excuses
- Demonstrate understanding of the impact
- Show genuine remorse
- Outline your plans for the future
- Express gratitude for the opportunity

What NOT to Include:

- Blaming others for your situation
- Minimizing the seriousness of the offense
- Making excuses rather than explanations
- Focusing only on consequences to you
- Generic statements that could apply to anyone

⚠ **APPLICATION STRATEGY**

Your application is your one chance to make a first impression. Work closely with your attorney to ensure your application presents your case in the strongest possible light. This isn't the time to be modest about your accomplishments or circumstances.

PROGRAM REQUIREMENTS AND EXPECTATIONS

Understanding what's expected helps you decide if diversion is right for you and prepares you for success.

Common Program Components

Drug Education Classes:

- Learn about addiction and its effects
- Understand the legal consequences of drug use
- Develop coping strategies and life skills
- Usually 8-16 hours of classroom time

Community Service:

- Unpaid work for approved organizations
- Typical range: 20-100 hours
- Must be completed within program timeframe
- Documentation required from supervising organization

Regular Drug Testing:

- Random urine, breath, or hair tests
- Zero tolerance for positive results
- Testing frequency varies by program
- Failed tests usually result in program termination

Check-in Meetings:

- Regular meetings with program coordinator
- Progress review and problem-solving
- Frequency ranges from weekly to monthly
- Attendance is mandatory

Treatment (if required):

- Substance abuse counseling
- Mental health treatment
- Medical care for addiction
- Compliance with treatment recommendations

Financial Costs

Program Fees:

- Administrative costs: $200-500
- Drug testing fees: $25-50 per test
- Education class fees: $100-300
- Treatment costs: Varies widely

Court Costs:

- Filing fees
- Administrative fees
- Restitution if applicable

Total Typical Cost: $500-2,000 depending on program requirements

SUCCESS STRATEGY CHECKLIST

Before Starting the Program:

- [ ] Understand all requirements clearly
- [ ] Budget for all costs involved
- [ ] Arrange work schedule around meetings
- [ ] Line up transportation to appointments
- [ ] Build support system of family/friends

During the Program:

- [ ] Attend all required meetings and classes
- [ ] Complete community service promptly
- [ ] Stay clean and pass all drug tests
- [ ] Maintain employment or education
- [ ] Keep detailed records of compliance

If Problems Arise:

- [ ] Contact program coordinator immediately
- [ ] Work with attorney to address issues
- [ ] Document any legitimate emergencies
- [ ] Never try to hide problems or violations

WHAT HAPPENS IF YOU SUCCEED

Successfully completing a diversion program opens doors that would otherwise be closed by a conviction.

Immediate Benefits

Charges Dismissed: Your criminal case is over with no conviction on your record.

Clean Record: You can truthfully say you've never been convicted of a crime.

Professional Licenses: Most licensing boards won't take action for dismissed charges.

Employment: No conviction to disclose on job applications.

Education: Continued eligibility for financial aid and educational programs.

Long-Term Advantages

Future Background Checks: Most background checks won't show dismissed charges.

Professional Growth: Career advancement isn't blocked by criminal convictions.

Personal Growth: Skills and insights gained during the program benefit your entire life.

Second Chance Validated: You've proven that one mistake doesn't define you.

Record Implications

What Shows Up: Some background checks may show the arrest but should show the charges were dismissed.

Expungement Options: You may be eligible to have the arrest record expunged after completing diversion.

Truthful Disclosure: You can honestly say you completed the program successfully and charges were dismissed.

WHAT HAPPENS IF YOU FAIL

Not everyone who enters diversion programs completes them successfully. Understanding the consequences helps you stay motivated.

Common Reasons for Failure

Failed Drug Tests: The most common cause of program termination.

Missed Appointments: Failing to attend required meetings or classes.

New Arrests: Any new criminal activity usually terminates the program.

Non-Payment: Failing to pay required fees or complete community service.

Non-Compliance: Not following specific program rules or requirements.

Consequences of Failure

Return to Regular Prosecution: Your case resumes as if diversion never happened.

No Credit for Partial Completion: Time and effort spent in the program generally don't count toward any sentence.

Statements May Be Used: Things you said during the program might be used against you.

Worse Plea Offers: Prosecutors may be less willing to negotiate after program failure.

SPECIAL CONSIDERATIONS FOR DIFFERENT SITUATIONS

Professional License Holders

Advantages of Diversion:

- Avoids conviction that triggers automatic licensing board action
- Demonstrates responsibility and commitment to change
- Preserves career and livelihood

Considerations:

- Some licensing boards review arrests even without convictions
- May need to disclose diversion participation
- Consult with licensing attorney in addition to criminal attorney

Non-Citizens

Immigration Benefits:

- Dismissed charges generally don't trigger immigration consequences
- Avoids conviction that could lead to deportation
- Preserves path to citizenship or status adjustment

Important Warning: Consult with immigration attorney before accepting any diversion program, as requirements might still affect immigration status.

Family Benefits:

- Keeps parent out of jail and available for children
- Preserves employment and family income
- Models responsibility and redemption for children

Considerations:

- Program requirements may affect family time
- Financial costs impact family budget
- Success depends on family support

NANCY'S REFLECTION

"Diversion was the best thing that happened to me during this whole ordeal. Yes, it required time and effort, but it gave me tools I never had before. I learned about addiction, stress management, and personal responsibility. Even though my legal case is over, I still use what I learned in the program every day."

FREQUENTLY ASKED QUESTIONS

Q Is diversion available in all Texas counties?

A No, diversion programs vary widely by county. Some counties have extensive programs while others have none. Your attorney can tell you what's available in your jurisdiction.

Q Can I apply for diversion if I have prior arrests but no convictions?

A Maybe. Policies vary by county, but some programs accept people with arrest histories if there were no convictions.

Q What happens if I move during the diversion program?

A This can be complicated. Some programs allow transfers to other counties, while others require completion in the original jurisdiction.

Q Can I appeal if I'm denied for diversion?

A Generally no. Diversion is discretionary, and prosecutors aren't required to offer it to anyone.

Q How long do I have to apply for diversion?

A Deadlines vary by county, but applications usually must be submitted early in the case, often within 30-60 days of charges being filed.

MAKING THE MOST OF YOUR SECOND CHANCE

If you're accepted into a diversion program, you're getting something precious: a genuine second chance. Here's how to make the most of it:

Take It Seriously: Treat the program as the opportunity it is, not as an inconvenience.

Address Root Causes: Use the program to deal with whatever led to your arrest in the first place.

Build Support Systems: Develop relationships and resources that will help you long after the program ends.

Document Your Success: Keep records of your compliance and achievements during the program.

Pay It Forward: Consider how you can help others who face similar challenges.

Stay Humble: Remember that this opportunity is a privilege, not a right.

Pretrial diversion programs represent the justice system at its best - recognizing that people can change, grow, and contribute positively to society after making mistakes. If you're offered this opportunity, embrace it fully. Your future self will thank you for the work you do today.

In the next chapter, we'll explore drug court programs - another avenue for treatment-focused justice that can transform lives while avoiding traditional criminal penalties.

CHAPTER 8: DRUG COURT AND TREATMENT PROGRAMS

When Nancy's attorney mentioned drug court as an option, she had mixed feelings. On one hand, it sounded like a way to avoid prison and get her life back on track. On the other hand, she'd heard it was really tough - lots of rules, constant supervision, and a huge time commitment. "Is it worth it?" she asked her lawyer. "That depends," he replied. "How serious are you about getting clean and staying clean?"

Here's the deal with drug court: it's not your typical court experience. Instead of just showing up, pleading guilty, and getting sentenced, you're entering into a partnership with the judge, your attorney, probation officers, and treatment counselors. Everyone's goal is the same - helping you beat your addiction and avoid future criminal charges. But this isn't a passive process where things just happen to you. You're going to be an active participant in your own recovery.

Think of drug court like an intensive, supervised treatment program that happens to be run through the court system. You'll have regular check-ins with the judge who will celebrate your successes and call you out when you're struggling. You'll attend counseling, submit to drug tests, and follow a structured program designed to address the root causes of your addiction. It's demanding, but thousands of Texans have successfully completed these programs and gotten their lives back. This chapter will walk you through exactly how drug court works and help you figure out if it's the right path for your situation.

DRUG COURT AT A GLANCE

What Drug Court Offers:

- ☐ Treatment-focused approach instead of punishment
- ☐ Reduced charges or sentences upon completion
- ☐ Intensive supervision and support
- ☐ Access to treatment resources
- ☐ Regular interaction with specialized judges

What Drug Court Requires:

- ☐ Admission of guilt or responsibility
- ☐ Commitment to treatment and recovery
- ☐ Regular court appearances (weekly/bi-weekly)
- ☐ Frequent drug testing
- ☐ Compliance with all program rules

HOW DRUG COURT WORKS

Drug courts operate differently from regular criminal courts. Understanding the structure helps you know what you're getting into.

The Drug Court Team

Drug Court Judge:

- Specially trained in addiction and treatment issues
- Takes an active role in your recovery process
- Has authority to impose sanctions or rewards
- Meets with you regularly to monitor progress

Treatment Coordinator:

- Assesses your treatment needs
- Connects you with appropriate services
- Monitors your compliance with treatment
- Reports progress to the court

Probation Officer:

- Supervises your compliance with court orders
- Conducts drug tests and home visits
- Provides support and accountability
- Can recommend sanctions for violations

Defense Attorney:

- Advocates for your interests throughout the program
- Helps you understand requirements and expectations
- Assists with any legal issues that arise
- Supports your success in the program

Prosecutor:

- Works collaboratively rather than adversarially
- Focuses on public safety and treatment success
- May recommend program modifications
- Supports successful participants

The Drug Court Process

Phase 1: Assessment and Stabilization (Months 1-4)

- Comprehensive addiction assessment
- Development of individualized treatment plan
- Weekly court appearances
- Intensive outpatient treatment begins
- Frequent drug testing (2-3 times per week)

Phase 2: Treatment and Skills Building (Months 5-8)

- Continued intensive treatment
- Bi-weekly court appearances
- Job training or educational programs
- Reduced drug testing frequency
- Development of recovery skills

Phase 3: Transition and Independence (Months 9-12)

- Monthly court appearances
- Transition to less intensive treatment
- Focus on employment and stability
- Continued drug testing
- Preparation for graduation

Phase 4: Maintenance and Graduation (Months 13+)

- Periodic court check-ins
- Minimal treatment requirements
- Demonstration of sustained recovery
- Planning for program completion
- Graduation ceremony

💡 **THE DRUG COURT DIFFERENCE**

Unlike traditional court, where you might see a judge for 5 minutes total over months of hearings, drug court judges get to know you personally. They celebrate your achievements, understand your struggles, and become invested in your success.

WHO QUALIFIES FOR DRUG COURT

Not everyone facing drug charges is eligible for drug court. Programs have specific criteria designed to identify participants most likely to succeed.

Common Eligibility Requirements

Addiction Diagnosis:

- Documented substance abuse or dependency
- Assessment by qualified professional
- Admission that addiction contributed to criminal behavior
- Willingness to undergo treatment

Criminal History:

- Usually limited to non-violent drug offenses
- Some programs accept people with minor prior convictions
- Serious violent crimes typically disqualify
- Weapons charges often exclude participation

Residency:

- Must live in or near the jurisdiction
- Stable housing or ability to obtain it
- Transportation to court and treatment
- Support system in the community

Motivation and Attitude:

- Genuine desire to overcome addiction
- Willingness to follow strict program rules
- Understanding of program expectations
- Commitment to complete all phases

Special Populations

Parents with Dependent Children:

- Many programs prioritize parents
- Family services may be included
- Childcare assistance sometimes available
- Family therapy components

Veterans:

- Some courts have specialized veteran tracks
- Address service-related trauma
- Connect with VA services
- Veteran mentors available

Young Adults:

- Special programs for 18-25 age group
- Focus on education and job training
- Peer support groups
- Family involvement encouraged

SIDEBAR: KEY TERMS

DRUG COURT:

Specialized court program that combines treatment with judicial supervision for substance-abusing offenders.

TREATMENT PLAN:

Individualized program addressing specific addiction and recovery needs.

SANCTIONS:

Consequences for program violations (jail time, increased requirements, etc.).

INCENTIVES:

Rewards for compliance and progress (reduced supervision, certificates, etc.).

RELAPSE:

Return to drug use during recovery (expected part of the process).

GRADUATION:

Successful completion of all drug court requirements.

AFTERCARE:

Ongoing support services after program completion.

THERAPEUTIC JURISPRUDENCE:

Legal approach focused on healing and rehabilitation rather than punishment.

PROGRAM REQUIREMENTS AND EXPECTATIONS

Drug court is intensive and demanding. Understanding what's required helps you prepare mentally and practically.

Court Appearances

Frequency:

- Weekly during Phase 1
- Bi-weekly during Phase 2
- Monthly in later phases
- Additional appearances for violations

What Happens:

- Check-in with judge about progress
- Discussion of any problems or successes
- Review of drug test results
- Sanctions or incentives imposed
- Planning for next phase

Expectations:

- Arrive on time and appropriately dressed
- Be honest about your struggles
- Accept responsibility for violations
- Show respect for the court process

Drug Testing

Frequency:

- 2-3 times per week initially
- Gradually reduced with good compliance
- Random scheduling
- Additional testing for suspicion

Types of Tests:

- Urine analysis (most common)
- Breath tests for alcohol
- Hair follicle testing
- Saliva tests

Zero Tolerance Policy:

- Any positive test is a violation
- Diluted samples treated as positive
- Missing tests counts as positive
- Prescription medications must be disclosed

Treatment Requirements

Assessment:

- Comprehensive evaluation by licensed professional
- Mental health screening
- Medical examination
- Development of treatment plan

Individual Counseling:

- Regular sessions with addiction counselor
- Address underlying issues
- Develop coping strategies
- Monitor progress and adjust treatment

Group Therapy:

- Peer support and accountability
- Learn from others' experiences
- Practice communication skills
- Build sober social network

Education Classes:

- Addiction education
- Life skills training
- Relapse prevention
- Vocational training

LIFE IN DRUG COURT: WHAT TO EXPECT

A Typical Week in Phase 1

Monday: Individual counseling session **Tuesday:** Drug test and check-in with probation officer **Wednesday:** Group therapy session **Thursday:** Drug test **Friday:** Court appearance with judge **Weekend:** NA/AA meetings and family time

The Emotional Journey

Early Stages:

- Anxiety about court appearances
- Adjustment to intensive schedule
- Withdrawal symptoms if applicable
- Hope mixed with uncertainty

Middle Stages:

- Developing routine and habits
- Building relationships with treatment team
- Experiencing ups and downs
- Learning new coping skills

Later Stages:

- Increased confidence and stability
- Focus on future planning
- Mentoring newer participants
- Preparing for life after graduation

⚠️ **REALITY CHECK**

Drug court is not easier than regular probation - it's actually much more intensive. If you're looking for a shortcut or easy way out, drug court isn't for you. It requires genuine commitment to change your life.

SANCTIONS AND INCENTIVES

Drug courts use a system of consequences and rewards to motivate compliance and progress.

Common Sanctions for Violations

Minor Violations:

- Additional court appearances
- Increased drug testing
- Community service hours
- Written assignments or essays
- Loss of privileges

Moderate Violations:

- Brief jail stays (1-3 days)
- Increased treatment requirements
- Earlier curfew times
- Electronic monitoring
- Starting phase over

Serious Violations:

- Longer jail sentences
- Termination from program
- Return to regular court process
- Enhanced charges
- Loss of plea agreement benefits

Incentives for Success

Phase Advancement:

- Moving to next program phase
- Reduced court appearances
- Less frequent drug testing
- Increased privileges

Recognition:

- Certificates of achievement
- Recognition in court
- Applause from court staff
- Positive entries in file

Practical Rewards:

- Bus passes or gas cards
- Gift certificates
- Reduced fees
- Early termination consideration

SUCCESS STRATEGIES

Before Entering Drug Court:

- [ ] Honestly assess your commitment level
- [ ] Discuss expectations with family
- [ ] Arrange work schedule flexibility
- [ ] Identify transportation options
- [ ] Begin addressing housing issues

During the Program:

- [ ] Attend every required appointment
- [ ] Be honest about struggles and relapses
- [ ] Build relationships with treatment team
- [ ] Use all available support services
- [ ] Focus on long-term goals, not just compliance

When Facing Challenges:

- [ ] Communicate problems immediately
- [ ] Ask for help before violating program rules
- [ ] Use relapse as learning opportunity
- [ ] Lean on your support network
- [ ] Remember why you started the program

SUCCESSFUL COMPLETION AND GRADUATION

Graduating from drug court is a significant achievement that opens many doors.

Graduation Requirements

Program Completion:

- Successfully complete all phases
- Maintain sustained sobriety (usually 6+ months)
- Meet all treatment goals
- Demonstrate stability in housing and employment

Court Obligations:

- Perfect attendance at required appearances
- Compliance with all court orders
- Payment of all fees and fines
- Completion of community service

Personal Growth:

- Development of relapse prevention plan
- Demonstration of life skills
- Establishment of sober support network
- Evidence of personal responsibility

Benefits of Graduation

Legal Benefits:

- Charges dismissed or significantly reduced
- Avoiding prison sentences
- Possible record sealing options
- Compliance with probation terms

Personal Benefits:

- Sustained recovery from addiction
- Improved relationships with family
- Better employment prospects
- Enhanced self-esteem and confidence
- Life skills for ongoing success

The Graduation Ceremony

Most drug courts hold formal graduation ceremonies to celebrate participants' achievements:

- Family and friends invited
- Recognition by judge and court staff
- Certificate of completion
- Speeches by graduates
- Celebration of transformation

WHAT HAPPENS IF YOU DON'T SUCCEED

Not everyone who enters drug court completes the program successfully. Understanding potential outcomes helps with decision-making.

Reasons for Termination

Repeated Violations:

- Multiple positive drug tests
- Consistent non-compliance
- Refusal to follow treatment recommendations
- Disruptive behavior in court

New Criminal Activity:

- Arrests for new offenses
- Violations that pose public safety risks
- Behavior incompatible with recovery

Voluntary Withdrawal:

- Deciding the program isn't right for you
- Moving out of jurisdiction
- Unable to meet time commitments

Consequences of Termination

Return to Regular Court:

- Face original charges
- Lose benefits of drug court plea agreement
- May receive harsher sentence
- Less favorable plea options

What You Keep:

- Treatment progress and insights
- Relationships built during program
- Skills learned in counseling
- Time already served may count toward sentence

SPECIAL CONSIDERATIONS

Employment and Drug Court

Time Commitment:

- Court appearances during business hours
- Treatment sessions may conflict with work
- Drug testing can be unpredictable

Disclosure to Employers:

- Some jobs require disclosure of court involvement
- Others may be understanding of recovery efforts
- Focus on commitment to treatment and change

Family Impact

Positive Effects:

- Family involvement in recovery process
- Improved relationships through sobriety
- Stability for children
- Support system development

Challenges:

- Time away from family for appointments
- Financial costs of program
- Stress of program requirements
- Adjustment to sober lifestyle

Financial Considerations

Program Costs:

- Court fees and fines
- Treatment costs
- Drug testing fees
- Transportation expenses

Total Investment: $2,000-$5,000 typically, but varies by program and individual needs

Long-term Savings: Avoiding conviction-related costs, maintaining employment, preventing future legal problems

💡 **GRADUATE PERSPECTIVE**

"Drug court saved my life. It wasn't easy - there were times I wanted to quit. But the judge never gave up on me, my counselor helped me understand my addiction, and my family saw me fighting to get better. Two years after graduation, I'm still sober and my life is completely different." - Former Drug Court Participant

FREQUENTLY ASKED QUESTIONS

Q **Can I work while in drug court?**

A Yes, employment is encouraged and often required. Programs work with participants to schedule around work commitments.

Q **What happens if I relapse during the program?**

A Relapse is often considered part of the recovery process. You'll face sanctions, but the goal is to learn from the experience and continue progressing.

Q **Can I travel while in drug court?**

A Travel requires advance permission and coordination with the court. Emergency travel may be accommodated with proper notification.

Q **How much does drug court cost?**

A Costs vary by program but typically include court fees, treatment costs, and drug testing fees. Some programs offer payment assistance.

Q **What if I can't complete all the phases?**

A Programs try to work with participants facing legitimate challenges. Communication with the court team is essential if you're struggling.

MAKING THE DRUG COURT DECISION

Drug court represents a significant commitment but offers the opportunity for genuine transformation. Consider these factors:

Choose Drug Court If:

- ☐ You're genuinely committed to overcoming addiction
- ☐ You have time and energy for intensive program requirements
- ☐ You want to address root causes, not just avoid punishment
- ☐ You're willing to be accountable and honest about your struggles

Consider Alternatives If:

- ☐ You're not ready to commit to sobriety
- ☐ You can't meet the time and attendance requirements
- ☐ You're looking for an easy way to avoid consequences
- ☐ You don't believe you have an addiction problem

Remember, drug court isn't just about avoiding jail - it's about transforming your life. If you're ready for that transformation, drug court can be the beginning of a completely different future.

In the next chapter, we'll explore plea bargains - the most common way drug cases are resolved and how to evaluate whether a plea offer is right for your situation.

CHAPTER 9: PLEA BARGAINS - UNDERSTANDING YOUR OPTIONS

Three months into her case, Nancy's attorney called with news: the prosecutor had made a plea offer. They were willing to reduce her felony charge to a misdemeanor in exchange for a guilty plea, probation, and completing a drug treatment program. Nancy's first instinct was relief - this sounded so much better than what she was originally facing. But then the questions started flooding in: Was this a good deal? Should she hold out for something better? What if she said no and they went to trial?

If you're facing a plea offer, you're probably having the same internal debate Nancy had. Plea bargains can feel like a blessing and a curse at the same time. On one hand, you get certainty and usually a better outcome than you'd face if convicted at trial. On the other hand, you're admitting guilt and accepting consequences when there's always a chance you could win your case completely.

Here's the thing about plea bargains: there's no universal "right" answer. What makes sense for one person might be terrible for another, depending on their circumstances, the strength of the evidence, and what they have to lose. The key is understanding exactly what you're being offered, what you're giving up, and what the alternatives look like. This chapter will help you evaluate plea offers like a pro, ask the right questions, and make the decision that's best for your specific situation. By the end, you'll know how to tell a good deal from a bad one.

📖 IF YOU ONLY READ ONE THING IN THIS CHAPTER

Never accept the first plea offer without letting your attorney investigate and negotiate. Ask these questions: (1) How does this compare to what I'm facing at trial? (2) How will this affect my job/family/future? (3) Can we get a better deal? Take time to think - most offers don't expire immediately.

PLEA BARGAIN EVALUATION CHECKLIST

Understanding the Offer:

- ☐ What exactly am I pleading guilty to?
- ☐ What's the recommended sentence?
- ☐ Are there any special conditions?
- ☐ What happens if I violate the terms?
- ☐ How does this affect my record long-term?

Comparing Alternatives:

- ☐ What's my maximum exposure if convicted at trial?
- ☐ How strong is the state's evidence?
- ☐ What are my chances of winning at trial?
- ☐ Are there other plea options available?
- ☐ Could I get a better deal later?

UNDERSTANDING PLEA BARGAINS

A plea bargain is essentially a contract between you and the state. You agree to plead guilty to specific charges, and the prosecutor agrees to recommend certain consequences.

Why Prosecutors Offer Plea Bargains

Guaranteed Conviction:

- Trials are uncertain - they might lose
- Plea bargains ensure a conviction
- Saves time and resources for both sides

Efficiency:

- Courts are overwhelmed with cases
- Trials take days or weeks
- Plea bargains can be resolved quickly

Victim Considerations:

- Avoids trauma of testifying
- Provides closure more quickly
- Guarantees some consequence for the defendant

Resource Management:

- Prosecutors can focus on more serious cases
- Saves taxpayer money
- Allows faster case resolution

Why Defendants Accept Plea Bargains

Reduced Charges:

- Felony reduced to misdemeanor
- Multiple charges reduced to fewer charges
- Lesser included offenses

Lighter Sentences:

- Probation instead of jail time
- Shorter jail sentences
- Reduced fines and fees

Certainty:

- Know exactly what consequences you're facing
- Avoid risk of harsher sentence after trial
- Can plan for the future

Faster Resolution:

- End the stress and uncertainty quickly
- Return to normal life sooner
- Avoid lengthy trial preparation

💡 THE REALITY OF PLEA BARGAINS

Over 95% of criminal cases end in plea bargains, not trials. This isn't because defendants are automatically guilty - it's because plea bargains often represent the most practical resolution for everyone involved.

TYPES OF PLEA AGREEMENTS

Not all plea bargains are the same. Understanding the different types helps you evaluate what you're being offered.

Charge Bargains

What It Means: Pleading guilty to a lesser charge than what you were originally charged with.

Examples:

- Felony possession reduced to misdemeanor possession
- Delivery charge reduced to simple possession
- Multiple charges reduced to single charge

Nancy's Situation: Her state jail felony was reduced to a Class A misdemeanor, eliminating the possibility of state jail time.

Benefits:

- Lower maximum punishment
- Less serious conviction on record
- Better long-term consequences

Sentence Bargains

What It Means: Pleading guilty to the original charge but with an agreed-upon sentence.

Examples:

- Agree to probation instead of jail time
- Specific jail sentence rather than range
- Deferred adjudication instead of regular probation

Benefits:

- Predictable outcome
- Often lighter than trial sentence
- Can include favorable terms

Count Bargains

What It Means: Pleading guilty to fewer charges when you're facing multiple counts.

Examples:

- Five possession charges reduced to one
- Delivery and possession charges reduced to possession only
- Enhanced charges dropped

Benefits:

- Reduced total exposure
- Simpler record
- Lower total punishment

Fact Bargains

What It Means: Agreeing to a specific version of events that results in lesser charges.

Examples:

- Agreeing amount was for personal use, not delivery
- Stipulating to facts that support lesser charges
- Agreeing to circumstances that reduce culpability

Caution: Be careful about agreeing to facts that aren't true or that you don't fully understand.

SIDEBAR: KEY TERMS

PLEA BARGAIN:

Agreement between prosecution and defense to resolve case without trial.

STIPULATION:

Agreed-upon facts that don't need to be proven at trial.

DEFERRED ADJUDICATION:

You plead guilty, but the judge doesn't enter a final conviction right away. If you complete probation successfully, the court will enter a no finding of guilt. If you violate probation, you can be sentenced to the full punishment range.

STRAIGHT PROBATION:

Regular probation with a final conviction.

TIME SERVED:

Credit for time already spent in jail applied to sentence.

CONCURRENT:

Multiple sentences served at the same time.

CONSECUTIVE:

Multiple sentences served one after another.

RESTITUTION:

Payment to victims for damages caused.

EVALUATING PLEA OFFERS

Deciding whether to accept a plea bargain requires careful analysis of multiple factors.

Strength of the State's Case

Strong State Case Indicators:

- Clear evidence of guilt
- Reliable witnesses
- Properly obtained evidence
- No significant constitutional issues

Weak State Case Indicators:

- Evidence problems or gaps
- Witness credibility issues
- Constitutional violations
- Chain of custody problems

How This Affects Plea Decisions: If the state's case is weak, you might get better offers or decide to go to trial. If it's strong, accepting a reasonable plea might be wise.

Your Personal Circumstances

Professional Considerations:

- Impact on professional licenses
- Employment consequences
- Security clearance issues
- Professional reputation

Family Factors:

- Time away from children

- Family financial stability
- Support system strength
- Impact on spouse/children

Immigration Status:

- Deportation consequences
- Path to citizenship affected
- Ability to return to U.S.
- Family reunification issues

Financial Reality:

- Cost of trial vs. plea
- Lost wages from jail time
- Fines and court costs
- Long-term financial impact

Risk Assessment

Trial Risks:

- Possibility of conviction on all charges
- Harsher sentence after trial
- Additional charges at trial
- Collateral consequences of trial

Plea Risks:

- Permanent criminal record
- Specific conditions you might violate
- Long-term consequences
- Giving up potential defenses

NEGOTIATING BETTER DEALS

Your attorney can often improve initial plea offers through skilled negotiation.

Timing of Negotiations

Early Negotiations:

- Based on limited information
- Often less favorable to defense
- Quick resolution possible
- Less attorney time and cost

Post-Discovery Negotiations:

- After reviewing all evidence
- Better understanding of case strength
- More informed decision-making
- Potentially better offers

Pre-Trial Negotiations:

- Final opportunity for deals
- Both sides motivated to avoid trial
- Most realistic assessments
- Often best offers available

Leverage in Negotiations

Defense Strengths:

- Evidence problems discovered
- Constitutional issues identified
- Witness credibility problems
- Prosecutor's heavy caseload

Mitigation Factors:

- First-time offender status
- Employment and family stability
- Community involvement
- Treatment already begun

Practical Considerations:

- Trial calendar congestion
- Witness availability issues
- Resource constraints
- Media or political pressure

⚠️ **NEGOTIATION REALITY**

Your attorney negotiates, but you decide. Never let anyone pressure you into accepting a plea bargain you're not comfortable with. Take time to understand all the implications before making this important decision.

SPECIAL TYPES OF PLEA AGREEMENTS

Deferred Adjudication

How It Works:

- Plead guilty or no contest
- Judge defers finding of guilt
- Complete probation successfully
- No finding of Guilt

Benefits:

- No final conviction if successful
- Eligible for non-disclosure in some cases
- Less severe long-term consequences
- Some professional licenses not affected

Risks:

- If you violate, can be sentenced up to maximum
- Still shows up on some background checks
- May not protect against all collateral consequences
- Violation consequences can be severe

Pretrial Intervention/Diversion

Different from Regular Plea:

- Charges dismissed upon completion
- No conviction at all
- Clean record result
- Often available to first-time offenders

Requirements:

- Admission of responsibility

- Completion of program requirements
- Payment of fees and costs
- Compliance with all conditions

Conditional Discharge

How It Works:

- Plead guilty to reduced charge
- Sentence suspended pending compliance
- Complete conditions successfully
- Conviction set aside or reduced

Common Conditions:

- Drug treatment completion
- Community service
- Regular drug testing
- Payment of costs

DECISION-MAKING FRAMEWORK

Questions to Ask Yourself:

About the Offer:

- ☐ Do I understand exactly what I'm agreeing to?
- ☐ Are the terms reasonable given my situation?
- ☐ Can I realistically comply with all conditions?
- ☐ How does this affect my long-term goals?

About Alternatives:

- ☐ What's my realistic chance of winning at trial?
- ☐ Could I get a better deal later?
- ☐ Is going to trial worth the additional risk?
- ☐ Do I have strong defenses to pursue?

About Consequences:

- ☐ How does this affect my job/career?
- ☐ What are the immigration implications?
- ☐ How will this impact my family?
- ☐ Can I live with this decision long-term?

COMMON PLEA BARGAIN MISTAKES

Accepting the First Offer

Why It's a Mistake: Initial offers are often just starting points in negotiations.

Better Approach: Let your attorney investigate and negotiate before making decisions.

Focusing Only on Jail Time

Why It's a Mistake: Other consequences can be more significant than jail time.

Better Approach: Consider all long-term implications, including professional, financial, and personal consequences.

Not Understanding the Deal

Why It's a Mistake: You're bound by what you agree to, even if you misunderstood.

Better Approach: Ask questions until you completely understand every aspect of the agreement.

Rushing the Decision

Why It's a Mistake: This is a life-changing decision that deserves careful consideration.

Better Approach: Take reasonable time to weigh all factors and discuss with family/attorney.

Ignoring Collateral Consequences

Why It's a Mistake: The criminal penalty is just one part of the total impact.

Better Approach: Consider effects on employment, licenses, immigration, housing, and other life areas.

THE PLEA HEARING PROCESS

Once you decide to accept a plea bargain, you'll have a formal plea hearing where the judge must accept your plea.

What Happens at the Plea Hearing

Judge's Inquiry:

- Confirms you understand the charges
- Verifies you understand your rights
- Ensures the plea is voluntary
- Reviews the plea agreement terms

Your Responses:

- Answer questions honestly
- Confirm your understanding
- State your plea clearly
- Acknowledge the consequences

Judge's Decision:

- Accepts or rejects the plea agreement
- Sets sentencing date if accepted
- Explains next steps in the process

Requirements for Valid Pleas

Knowing and Intelligent:

- You understand the charges and consequences
- You've been advised of your rights
- You comprehend what you're giving up

Voluntary:

- No coercion or improper pressure
- Adequate time to consider decision
- Competent to make the decision

Factual Basis:

- Evidence supports the charges you're pleading to
- Your conduct fits the legal requirements
- Court is satisfied guilt can be proven

AFTER ACCEPTING A PLEA BARGAIN

If You Get Probation

Compliance is Critical:

- Follow all terms exactly
- Report as required
- Pay fees on time
- Avoid new arrests

Benefits of Success:

- Complete sentence without jail time
- Maintain employment and family stability
- Demonstrate responsibility and rehabilitation
- Move forward with your life

If You Get Jail Time

Time Served Credit:

- Credit for time spent in jail before sentencing
- May reduce actual time to serve
- Can sometimes result in immediate release

Preparing for Incarceration:

- Arrange family and work matters
- Understand jail rules and procedures
- Plan for release and reintegration
- Maintain positive attitude and use time constructively

NANCY'S DECISION

"After my attorney explained all my options, I decided to accept the plea bargain reducing my felony to a misdemeanor. Yes, I'd have a conviction, but after a thorough review, it appeared that this solution would keep my nursing license safe and avoided jail time. Looking back, it was the right choice for my situation."

FREQUENTLY ASKED QUESTIONS

Q Can I change my mind after accepting a plea bargain?

A Generally no, once the judge accepts your plea. There are very limited circumstances where plea withdrawal might be allowed.

Q What if the judge rejects our plea agreement?

A You can usually withdraw your plea and go to trial, or try to negotiate a different agreement the judge will accept.

Q Do I have to accept any plea offer?

A Absolutely not. You have the right to reject any offer and go to trial.

Q Can plea negotiations continue even after I reject an offer?

A Yes, negotiations can continue up until trial, though offers may become less favorable over time.

Q What if I can't afford the fines in the plea agreement?

A Most courts offer payment plans or community service alternatives. Discuss options with your attorney.

MAKING YOUR DECISION

Deciding whether to accept a plea bargain is one of the most important choices you'll make in your case. Consider these final thoughts:

Accept a Plea Bargain When:

- ☐ The offer is significantly better than trial risks
- ☐ Evidence against you is strong
- ☐ You want certainty and closure
- ☐ Trial costs outweigh potential benefits
- ☐ The deal allows you to move forward with your life

Consider Going to Trial When:

- ☐ You're truly innocent and can prove it
- ☐ The state's case has serious weaknesses
- ☐ The plea offer isn't much better than trial consequences
- ☐ Constitutional issues might get evidence suppressed
- ☐ You cannot live with having a conviction

Remember, there's no shame in accepting a reasonable plea bargain. The goal isn't to "win" or "lose" - it's to achieve the best possible outcome for your specific situation. Your attorney can provide guidance, but ultimately this decision is yours to make.

In the next chapter, we'll explore what happens if you decide to go to trial - the process, what to expect, and how to prepare for this significant undertaking.

CHAPTER 10:

GOING TO TRIAL

WHAT TO EXPECT

DON'T STRESS ABOUT THIS YET

Most drug cases (over 95%) end in plea bargains, not trials. If you're reading this in your first few weeks after arrest, focus on Chapters 1-5 first. You may never need the information in this chapter, but it's here if your case heads to trial.

What if Nancy had ultimately decided to reject the plea offer and take her case to trial. Her attorney had found some problems with the search that led to her arrest, and they believed they had a real chance of winning. Still, as the trial date approached, Nancy felt nervous about putting her fate in the hands of strangers. "What if the jury doesn't like me?" she worried. Her attorney smiled and said, "Nancy, you're going to do just fine. We've prepared for this, and we know exactly what we're doing."

If your case is heading to trial, you need to know something important: you are not powerless in this process. Yes, trials can feel intimidating when you've never been through one before, but they're not the unpredictable free-for-alls you see on TV. Trials follow specific rules and procedures, and your attorney knows how to navigate every step. You have constitutional rights that protect you throughout the process, and the burden is entirely on the state to prove you're guilty beyond a reasonable doubt.

You chose to go to trial for a reason - maybe the evidence against you is weak, maybe the police made mistakes, or maybe you simply refuse to plead guilty to something you didn't do. Whatever your reason, you have every right to make the state prove their case, and thousands of people win their trials every year in Texas. This chapter will walk you through exactly what happens from jury selection to verdict, so you'll know what to expect and can participate confidently in your own defense. You're not just along for the ride - you're fighting for your future, and you have every tool you need to win.

TRIAL PREPARATION CHECKLIST

Before Trial Begins:

- [ ] Understand the charges and potential penalties
- [ ] Review key evidence with your attorney
- [ ] Prepare for testimony (if you plan to testify)
- [ ] Arrange time off work for trial duration
- [ ] Plan for family and childcare needs
- [ ] Prepare appropriate courtroom attire

During Trial:

- [ ] Arrive early and dress professionally
- [ ] Follow courtroom etiquette
- [ ] Stay calm and composed
- [ ] Listen carefully to all proceedings
- [ ] Take notes if helpful
- [ ] Trust your attorney's strategy

UNDERSTANDING YOUR CONSTITUTIONAL RIGHTS AT TRIAL

Your rights don't disappear when you go to trial - in fact, they become even more important.

Presumption of Innocence

What It Means: You are presumed innocent until proven guilty beyond a reasonable doubt.

Practical Impact:

- The state must prove every element of the charge
- You don't have to prove your innocence
- Doubt should be resolved in your favor
- The jury starts with the assumption you're innocent

Burden of Proof

Beyond a Reasonable Doubt: The highest standard in our legal system.

What This Means:

- More than "probably guilty"
- More than "likely guilty"
- The evidence must be so convincing that a reasonable person would not hesitate to rely on it
- If there's reasonable doubt, you must be found not guilty

Right to Remain Silent

You Cannot Be Forced to Testify: The decision whether to testify is entirely yours.

Prosecution Cannot Comment: They can't tell the jury that your silence means you're guilty.

Strategic Considerations: Your attorney will help you decide whether testifying helps or hurts your case.

Right to Confront Witnesses

Cross-Examination: Your attorney can question every witness against you.

Face Your Accusers: Witnesses must testify in person, not through written statements.

Challenge Credibility: Your attorney can expose lies, inconsistencies, and bias.

💡 **YOUR TRIAL ADVANTAGES**

You start ahead: The jury begins with the assumption that you are innocent. The state has to convince them otherwise with strong evidence. If they fail to meet this high burden, you win.

JURY SELECTION: CHOOSING THE PEOPLE WHO WILL DECIDE

Jury selection (called "voir dire") is often the most important part of your trial.

Understanding Texas Jury Composition

Felony Cases: 12 jurors who must reach a unanimous verdict

Misdemeanor Cases: 6 jurors who must reach a unanimous verdict

Alternates: Additional jurors selected in case regular jurors can't continue

The Voir Dire Process

Initial Questioning:

- Judge asks basic questions about eligibility
- Attorneys ask about attitudes and experiences
- Jurors answer questions about their backgrounds
- Potential biases are explored

Challenges for Cause:

- Removing jurors who can't be fair
- No limit on these challenges
- Must show clear bias or inability to follow law

Peremptory Challenges:

- Limited number of challenges without stating reasons
- Strategic removal of unfavorable jurors
- Cannot be based on race or gender

What Your Attorney Looks For

Favorable Juror Characteristics:

- Open-minded about police mistakes
- Understanding of addiction issues
- Experience with unfair treatment
- Skeptical of authority
- Critical thinking skills

Unfavorable Characteristics:

- Strong law-and-order attitudes
- Blind trust in police testimony
- Harsh views on drug offenses
- Inability to presume innocence
- Personal experience as crime victims

SIDEBAR: KEY TERMS

VOIR DIRE:

Jury selection process where potential jurors are questioned.

VENIRE:

The pool of potential jurors called for selection.

CHALLENGE FOR CAUSE:

Removing a juror who cannot be fair or follow the law.

PEREMPTORY CHALLENGE:

Removing a juror without stating a reason (limited number available).

UNANIMOUS VERDICT:

All jurors must agree on guilt or innocence.

HUNG JURY:

When jurors cannot reach a unanimous verdict.

MISTRIAL:

Trial ended without a verdict due to procedural problems or hung jury.

BURDEN OF PROOF:

Prosecution's obligation to prove guilt beyond a reasonable doubt.

THE TRIAL PROCESS: STEP BY STEP

Understanding the trial sequence helps you know what to expect each day.

Opening Statements

Prosecution Goes First:

- Outlines their case and evidence
- Tells their version of events
- Explains what they intend to prove
- Not evidence, just a preview

Defense Opening:

- May present immediately or wait until after state's case
- Challenges prosecution's theory
- Highlights weaknesses in state's case
- Explains defense strategy

Your Role: Listen carefully but remember these are just statements, not evidence.

State's Case-in-Chief

Prosecution Presents Evidence:

- Calls witnesses to testify
- Introduces physical evidence
- Plays recordings or videos
- Presents lab reports and expert testimony

Cross-Examination:

- Your attorney questions each witness
- Challenges testimony and evidence

- Exposes inconsistencies and bias
- Highlights favorable facts

Evidence Rules:

- Only relevant, reliable evidence allowed
- Your attorney can object to improper evidence
- Judge decides what jury can hear

Motion for Directed Verdict

After State's Case:

- Defense can argue state failed to prove case
- Rarely granted but preserves issues for appeal
- Judge evaluates whether any reasonable jury could convict

Defense Case (Optional)

Your Choice: You're not required to present any evidence.

If You Present a Defense:

- Call witnesses favorable to your case
- Present evidence that contradicts state's case
- Challenge state's evidence with experts
- Tell your side of the story

Strategic Considerations:

- Sometimes the state's case is so weak that presenting evidence is unnecessary
- Other times, you need to provide alternative explanations
- Your attorney will advise based on how the trial is going

YOUR OPTIONS FOR TESTIFYING

One of the biggest decisions in any trial is whether you should testify in your own defense.

Reasons to Testify

Your Story Needs Telling:

- Only you can explain your actions
- Provide context for your behavior
- Contradict prosecution witnesses
- Show your character and credibility

Jury Expectations:

- Some jurors expect to hear from defendants
- Your silence might be misinterpreted despite jury instructions
- Personal testimony can be powerful

Strong Alibi or Defense:

- You have clear evidence of innocence
- You can provide a compelling alternative explanation
- Your version of events is well-supported

Reasons Not to Testify

Cross-Examination Risks:

- Prosecutor will attack your credibility
- Prior bad acts might be revealed
- Inconsistencies will be highlighted
- You might say something damaging

State's Case is Weak:

- Why give them a chance to strengthen their case?

- Your silence can't be used against you
- Let reasonable doubt do the work

Preparation Concerns:

- Testifying requires extensive preparation
- Some people don't perform well under pressure
- Nervousness can appear as dishonesty

⚠ TESTIFYING DECISION

This choice is yours alone. Your attorney can advise you, but they cannot make this decision for you. Consider all factors carefully and don't let anyone pressure you either way.

WHAT MAKES A STRONG DEFENSE

Effective trial defenses in drug cases often focus on these key areas:

Challenging the Search and Seizure

Fourth Amendment Violations:

- Unlawful traffic stops
- Searches without consent or warrants
- Exceeding scope of consent
- Coercive police tactics

Suppression Motions:

- Filed before trial to exclude evidence
- Heard by judge, not jury
- Can eliminate key evidence
- Sometimes end cases entirely

Attacking the Evidence

Chain of Custody Problems:

- Gaps in evidence handling
- Unauthorized access to evidence
- Improper storage conditions
- Missing documentation

Lab Analysis Issues:

- Equipment malfunctions
- Technician errors
- Contamination problems
- Lack of proper procedures

Credibility Challenges

Police Officer Testimony:

- Inconsistencies in reports
- Memory problems
- Bias or misconduct
- Training deficiencies

Witness Problems:

- Motivation to lie
- Poor memory or observation
- Substance abuse issues
- Plea deals with prosecution

Factual Defenses

Lack of Knowledge:

- Didn't know drugs were present
- Drugs belonged to someone else
- No knowledge of illegal nature

Lack of Possession:

- Not in your control
- Temporary or brief contact
- Constructive possession challenges

THE PROSECUTION'S STRATEGY

Understanding how prosecutors approach drug trials helps you prepare for their tactics.

Building Their Case

Scientific Evidence:

- Lab results showing illegal substances
- Chain of custody documentation
- Expert testimony about testing
- Photos and physical evidence

Witness Testimony:

- Arresting officers
- Laboratory technicians
- Other witnesses to events
- Cooperating co-defendants

Circumstantial Evidence:

- Your behavior during arrest
- Statements you made
- Items found with drugs
- Location and circumstances

Common Prosecution Arguments

"The Evidence Speaks for Itself":

- Focus on physical evidence
- Minimize need for complex explanations
- Rely on lab results and officer testimony

“Defendant’s Behavior Shows Guilt”:

- Nervous behavior during stop
- Attempts to hide or flee
- Inconsistent statements
- Failure to cooperate

Prosecution Weaknesses to Exploit

Over-Reliance on Police Testimony:

- Officers may have poor memory
- Reports written days after events
- Pressure to make arrests
- Training inadequacies

Scientific Evidence Problems:

- Lab backlogs and rushed work
- Equipment not properly maintained
- Chain of custody gaps
- Contamination possibilities

TRIAL DAY SURVIVAL GUIDE

What to Wear:

- Business attire (suit if possible)
- Conservative colors
- Clean and pressed clothing
- Minimal jewelry
- No visible tattoos if possible

How to Behave:

- Arrive early every day
- Stand when judge enters
- No talking during proceedings
- No visible reactions to testimony
- Take notes if it helps you focus

What to Bring:

- Legal pad for notes
- Tissues
- Contact information for family
- Snacks for breaks
- Phone charger

What NOT to Do:

- Don't discuss case in courthouse
- Don't use social media about trial
- Don't coach family members who might testify
- Don't show emotion to jury reactions
- Don't interrupt or talk to your attorney during proceedings

CLOSING ARGUMENTS: THE FINAL PITCH

After all evidence is presented, both sides get to make closing arguments.

Prosecution's Closing

Summarizing Evidence:

- Reviews testimony and physical evidence
- Connects evidence to elements of charges
- Addresses defense arguments
- Asks for conviction

Emotional Appeals:

- Emphasizes harm caused by drugs
- Appeals to law and order
- Minimizes defendant's personal circumstances

Defense Closing

Reasonable Doubt Focus:

- Highlights weaknesses in state's case
- Points out inconsistencies
- Emphasizes burden of proof
- Argues for acquittal

Alternative Explanations:

- Provides innocent explanations for evidence
- Challenges state's interpretation
- Humanizes defendant
- Appeals for fairness

Prosecution Rebuttal

Final Word:

- Prosecution gets last chance to speak
- Can only respond to defense arguments
- Cannot introduce new theories
- Final appeal to convict

JURY DELIBERATIONS AND VERDICT

After closing arguments, the jury deliberates in private to reach their verdict.

The Deliberation Process

Judge's Instructions:

- Explains the law that applies
- Defines elements of charges
- Explains burden of proof
- Gives procedural guidance

Jury's Task:

- Review all evidence presented
- Apply law to facts
- Reach unanimous decision
- May ask questions or review evidence

Timeline:

- Can take hours or days
- No time limit in most cases
- Jury can request breaks
- Judge may encourage continued deliberation

Possible Verdicts

Guilty:

- Unanimous agreement on guilt
- Leads to sentencing phase
- Appeal rights preserved

Not Guilty:

- Unanimous agreement on innocence
- Case completely over
- Cannot be retried for same offense

Hung Jury:

- Cannot reach unanimous verdict
- Results in mistrial
- State can choose to retry case

IF YOU WIN:
COMPLETE VICTORY

IMMEDIATE FREEDOM:

You walk out of court completely free.

NO CRIMINAL RECORD:

The charges are permanently dismissed.

NO COLLATERAL CONSEQUENCES:

Professional licenses, immigration status, and other areas of your life are unaffected.

VINDICATION:

You've been found innocent by a jury of your peers.

MOVING FORWARD:

You can truthfully say you were never convicted of a crime.

IF YOU LOSE: THE PUNISHMENT PHASE

In Texas, if you're convicted, there's a separate hearing to determine your punishment.

Punishment Evidence

State May Present:

- Your criminal history
- Evidence of character
- Impact on victims
- Aggravating circumstances

Defense May Present:

- Character witnesses
- Family circumstances
- Employment history
- Mitigating factors
- Evidence of rehabilitation

Sentencing Options

Probation:

- Community supervision instead of jail
- Available for most drug offenses
- Requires compliance with conditions

Jail/Prison Time:

- Within statutory range for offense
- Credit for time already served
- Possibility of parole

Fines and Costs:

- Court costs and fees
- Restitution if applicable
- Payment plans available

FREQUENTLY ASKED QUESTIONS

Q How long do drug trials typically last?

A Simple possession cases might be completed in 1-2 days, while complex cases can take a week or more.

Q Can family members attend my trial?

A Yes, trials are public proceedings. Family support can be helpful, but they must follow courtroom rules.

Q What if I'm found guilty of a lesser charge than I was originally charged with?

A The jury can find you guilty of any included offense, which might be better than the original charge.

Q Can I change my mind and accept a plea deal during trial?

A Possibly, but the prosecutor isn't required to keep offers open once trial begins.

Q What happens if there's a mistrial?

A The prosecutor can choose to retry your case, offer a plea deal, or dismiss charges.

MAKING THE TRIAL DECISION

Going to trial is a significant decision that should be based on careful analysis:

Consider Trial When:

- [ ] The state's evidence is weak
- [ ] You have strong constitutional defenses
- [ ] The plea offers aren't significantly better than trial risk
- [ ] You're truly innocent and can prove it
- [ ] You cannot live with a conviction

Consider Plea Bargaining When:

- [ ] The evidence against you is strong
- [ ] The plea offer is significantly better than trial risk
- [ ] You want certainty and closure
- [ ] Trial costs outweigh potential benefits
- [ ] The collateral consequences of conviction are manageable

Remember, the decision to go to trial is ultimately yours. Your attorney can provide guidance about the strength of your case and the risks involved, but you're the one who has to live with the consequences. Choose the path that gives you the best chance of achieving your goals while allowing you to sleep at night knowing you made the right decision for your situation.

In the next chapter, we'll explore sentencing and punishment ranges in Texas, so yvou understand exactly what you might be facing whether you go to trial or accept a plea bargain.

CHAPTER 11: SENTENCING AND PUNISHMENT RANGES IN TEXAS

If you're facing sentencing - whether after a trial or as part of a plea agreement - you're probably feeling just as anxious as Nancy was. The uncertainty is probably the worst part. You know you're going to face consequences, but not knowing exactly what those consequences will be can drive you crazy. Here's some good news: sentencing in Texas isn't random, and judges don't just make up punishments on the spot.

Texas has specific punishment ranges for every type of drug offense, and there are rules about who's eligible for probation versus prison time. While judges do have some discretion within those ranges, they consider predictable factors like your criminal history, the circumstances of your offense, and evidence about your character and background. Understanding how sentencing works takes a lot of the mystery out of the process and helps you prepare for what's coming. This chapter will break down exactly how judges make these decisions and what you can do to influence the outcome in your favor.

SENTENCING PREPARATION CHECKLIST

Documents to Gather:

- ☐ Employment records and references
- ☐ Educational transcripts and certificates
- ☐ Character reference letters
- ☐ Community service documentation
- ☐ Treatment program records
- ☐ Financial records showing dependents

People to Contact:

- ☐ Family members willing to testify
- ☐ Employers or supervisors
- ☐ Community leaders or clergy
- ☐ Treatment counselors
- ☐ Character witnesses

Personal Preparation:

- ☐ Prepare statement of remorse (if appropriate)
- ☐ Plan for potential outcomes
- ☐ Arrange family support
- ☐ Understand probation conditions

UNDERSTANDING TEXAS PUNISHMENT RANGES

Texas law sets specific punishment ranges for each level of offense. Knowing these ranges helps you understand what you're facing.

Misdemeanor Penalties

Class C Misdemeanor:

- Fine up to $500
- No jail time
- Examples: Small amounts of marijuana paraphernalia

Class B Misdemeanor:

- Up to 180 days in jail
- Fine up to $2,000
- Examples: Marijuana under 2 ounces

Class A Misdemeanor:

- Up to 1 year in jail
- Fine up to $4,000
- Examples: Marijuana 2-4 ounces, small amounts of certain prescription drugs

Felony Penalties

State Jail Felony:

- 180 days to 2 years in state jail
- Fine up to $10,000
- Examples: Small amounts of Penalty Group 1 drugs, marijuana 4 ounces to 5 pounds

Third Degree Felony:

- 2 to 10 years in prison
- Fine up to $10,000
- Examples: Penalty Group 1 drugs 1-4 grams, marijuana 5-50 pounds

Second Degree Felony:

- 2 to 20 years in prison
- Fine up to $10,000
- Examples: Penalty Group 1 drugs 4-200 grams

First Degree Felony:

- 5 to 99 years in prison
- Fine up to $10,000
- Examples: Penalty Group 1 drugs 200-400 grams

Enhanced First Degree Felony:

- 15 to 99 years in prison
- Fine up to $10,000
- Examples: Penalty Group 1 drugs over 400 grams

UNDERSTANDING RANGES

Punishment ranges show the legal limits, not what you'll necessarily receive. Factors like your criminal history, the specific circumstances, and mitigation evidence significantly influence where within that range your sentence falls.

FACTORS THAT INFLUENCE SENTENCING

Judges consider many factors when determining your specific sentence within the legal range.

Your Criminal History

First-Time Offenders:

- Generally receive lighter sentences
- Often eligible for probation
- May qualify for deferred adjudication
- Considered lower risk for reoffending

Prior Misdemeanor Convictions:

- May affect eligibility for certain programs
- Can influence judge's perception of likelihood to reoffend
- Generally less impactful than felony convictions

Prior Felony Convictions:

- Can enhance your punishment range
- May make probation unavailable
- Significantly influences judge's sentencing decision
- Habitual offender laws may apply

Circumstances of the Current Offense

Aggravating Factors:

- Large quantities of drugs
- Evidence of dealing or distribution
- Weapons present during offense

- Offense near schools or youth centers
- Involvement of minors

Mitigating Factors:

- Small amounts for personal use
- Evidence of addiction rather than dealing
- Cooperation with law enforcement
- Immediate acceptance of responsibility
- Efforts at treatment before sentencing

Personal Circumstances

Employment and Stability:

- Steady employment history
- Current job situation
- Skills and education
- Financial responsibility

Family Responsibilities:

- Dependent children
- Caregiver roles
- Family support system
- Impact of incarceration on family

Community Ties:

- Length of residence
- Community involvement
- Volunteer work
- Religious or organizational participation

SIDEBAR: KEY TERMS

PUNISHMENT RANGE:

The minimum and maximum penalties allowed by law for each offense level.

ENHANCEMENT:

Legal mechanism that increases punishment ranges based on prior convictions.

HABITUAL OFFENDER:

Repeat felon subject to increased punishment ranges.

MITIGATION:

Evidence presented to reduce the severity of punishment.

AGGRAVATION:

Evidence presented to increase the severity of punishment.

DEFERRED ADJUDICATION:

Type of probation where final conviction is deferred.

STRAIGHT PROBATION:

Regular probation with immediate final conviction.

TIME SERVED:

Credit given for time spent in jail before sentencing.

ENHANCEMENT AND HABITUAL OFFENDER LAWS

Texas has strict laws that increase punishments for repeat offenders.

How Enhancement Works

Previous State Jail Felony:

- Can enhance a new state jail felony to a third degree felony
- Minimum punishment increases significantly

Previous Third Degree Felony:

- Can enhance a new felony to a second degree felony
- Reduces probation eligibility

Previous Second Degree Felony:

- Can enhance a new felony to a first degree felony
- May eliminate probation eligibility

Habitual Offender Status

Two Prior Felonies:

- Third felony can mean 25 years to life in prison
- Judge has some choice, but minimum is 25 years
- Makes it much harder to get parole

Three or More Prior Felonies:

- Can result in life sentence
- Extremely limited parole eligibility
- Reserved for most serious repeat offenders

Drug-Free Zone Enhancements

Location-Based Penalties:

- Offenses within 1,000 feet of schools, playgrounds, or youth centers
- Can bump misdemeanors to felonies
- Increases punishment ranges for felonies
- Prosecution must prove location and distance

Common Drug-Free Zones:

- Elementary and secondary schools
- Playgrounds and youth centers
- Public swimming pools
- Video arcade facilities

PROBATION ELIGIBILITY

Understanding when probation is available helps you plan your sentencing strategy.

Automatic Probation Eligibility

First-Time Offenders:

- Most drug charges are probation-eligible for first-time felons
- Judge cannot deny probation for first felony conviction
- Includes both straight probation and deferred adjudication

Specific Offense Eligibility:

- Most drug possession charges
- Many delivery charges under certain amounts
- Non-violent drug offenses

Factors That May Limit Probation

Prior Criminal History:

- Previous felony convictions may eliminate automatic eligibility
- Multiple prior convictions make probation unlikely
- Recent probation violations

Offense Circumstances:

- Large amounts suggesting distribution
- Use of weapons
- Involvement of minors
- Violence associated with offense

Types of Probation

Deferred Adjudication:

- Judge defers finding of guilt
- Successful completion can result in a no finding of guilt
- Violation can result in full punishment range
- Often preferred by defendants

Straight Probation:

- Immediate conviction and probation
- Cannot be enhanced if violated
- Punishment limited to original range
- Sometimes required by prosecutors

⚠️ PROBATION REALITY

Being eligible for probation doesn't guarantee you'll get it. Judges consider many factors beyond legal eligibility. Present the strongest possible case for why probation serves justice better than incarceration.

BUILDING YOUR MITIGATION CASE

The evidence you present at sentencing can significantly influence the judge's decision.

Character Evidence

Employment History:

- Steady work record
- Current employer support
- Skills and education
- Financial responsibility

Family Relationships:

- Spouse and children who depend on you
- Caregiver responsibilities
- Strong family support
- Impact of incarceration on family

Community Involvement:

- Volunteer work
- Religious participation
- Community organizations
- Mentoring or helping others

Demonstrating Change

Treatment Efforts:

- Voluntary enrollment in treatment
- Completion of programs
- Ongoing counseling
- Sponsor relationships in recovery programs

Education and Self-Improvement:

- GED or college completion
- Vocational training
- Professional development
- Personal growth efforts

Acceptance of Responsibility:

- Genuine remorse for actions
- Understanding of impact on others
- Commitment to making amends
- Realistic plans for the future

MITIGATION EVIDENCE CHECKLIST

Character Reference Letters:

- ☐ Current employer or supervisor
- ☐ Long-time friends (not co-defendants)
- ☐ Community leaders or clergy
- ☐ Teachers or mentors
- ☐ Family members
- ☐ Treatment counselors

Documentation:

- ☐ Employment records and evaluations
- ☐ Educational transcripts
- ☐ Military service records
- ☐ Treatment completion certificates
- ☐ Community service records
- ☐ Awards or recognitions

Witness Testimony:

- ☐ Family members explaining impact
- ☐ Employers supporting continued employment
- ☐ Treatment professionals discussing progress
- ☐ Community members attesting to character

THE SENTENCING HEARING PROCESS

Understanding what happens at sentencing helps you prepare mentally and strategically.

Pre-Sentence Investigation

Probation Department Report:

- Background investigation
- Criminal history verification
- Family and employment information
- Recommendation to court

Your Input:

- Interview with probation officer
- Opportunity to provide information
- Documentation you want considered
- Corrections to inaccurate information

The Sentencing Hearing

State's Presentation:

- Evidence supporting harsher sentence
- Impact statements from victims
- Your criminal history
- Aggravating circumstances

Defense Presentation:

- Character witnesses
- Mitigation evidence

- Treatment and rehabilitation efforts
- Plans for the future

Your Statement:

- Opportunity to address the court
- Express remorse (if genuine)
- Explain circumstances
- Request specific sentence

Judge's Decision:

- Reviews all evidence presented
- Considers legal requirements
- Announces sentence
- Explains reasoning

PREPARING YOUR STATEMENT TO THE COURT

If you choose to speak at sentencing, preparation is crucial.

What to Include

Accept Responsibility:

- Acknowledge your actions
- Don't make excuses
- Show genuine remorse
- Understand impact on others

Demonstrate Change:

- Describe steps you've taken
- Explain what you've learned
- Show commitment to different choices
- Outline plans for the future

Request Specific Outcome:

- Ask for probation if appropriate
- Request treatment opportunities
- Explain why incarceration isn't necessary
- Show you can be productive in community

What to Avoid

Making Excuses:

- Blaming others for your actions
- Minimizing seriousness of offense
- Claiming unfair treatment
- Arguing about the law or evidence

Appearing Insincere:

- Generic statements that could apply to anyone
- Reading something obviously written by attorney
- Showing no emotion or too much emotion
- Focusing only on consequences to you

ALTERNATIVE SENTENCING OPTIONS

Texas offers several alternatives to traditional incarceration for appropriate cases.

Treatment-Based Sentences

Residential Treatment:

- In-patient drug or alcohol treatment
- Serves sentence while receiving care
- Addresses underlying addiction issues
- Often shorter than prison time

Intensive Outpatient Programs:

- Maintains employment and family connections
- Regular counseling and group sessions
- Frequent drug testing
- Court supervision

Community-Based Alternatives

Community Service:

- Unpaid work for nonprofit organizations
- Serves community while avoiding incarceration
- Can be combined with other penalties
- Demonstrates commitment to making amends

Electronic Monitoring:

- House arrest with GPS monitoring
- Maintains employment opportunities
- Keeps families together
- Significantly cheaper than incarceration

Weekend Confinement:

- Serve sentence on weekends only
- Maintains employment during week
- Gradual completion of sentence
- Family stability maintained

UNDERSTANDING YOUR SENTENCE

Once sentenced, understand exactly what your punishment entails.

Probation Terms

Standard Conditions:

- Report to probation officer as directed
- Pay all fines, fees, and court costs
- Perform community service if ordered
- Avoid contact with law enforcement
- Stay within authorized geographic area

Special Conditions:

- Drug testing and treatment
- Counseling requirements
- No alcohol consumption
- Curfew restrictions
- No contact with certain people

Incarceration Details

Credit for Time Served:

- Time in jail before sentencing counts
- Can significantly reduce actual time served
- Sometimes results in immediate release

Parole Eligibility:

- Most sentences allow parole consideration
- Actual time served often less than sentence
- Good behavior affects parole decisions

Sentence Completion:

- Understanding when sentence ends
- Requirements for successful completion
- Effect on future criminal history

NANCY'S SENTENCING OUTCOME

"I was terrified about sentencing, but my attorney had prepared a strong mitigation package. The judge followed the negotiated plea agreement and sentenced me to two years deferred adjudication probation. I had to complete treatment and community service, but I kept my job and my nursing license. The preparation made all the difference."

FREQUENTLY ASKED QUESTIONS

Q **Can a judge sentence me to more than the plea agreement recommends?**

A In most cases, judges follow plea agreement recommendations, but they're not absolutely required to do so.

Q **What if I can't afford the fines in my sentence?**

A Most courts offer payment plans or community service alternatives. Communicate with your probation officer about financial hardships.

Q **Can I appeal my sentence if I think it's too harsh?**

A You can appeal sentences that exceed legal limits, but judges have broad discretion within punishment ranges.

Q **How long do I have to report to probation after sentencing?**

A Usually within 24-48 hours, but your attorney will get specific instructions from the court.

Q **What happens if I violate probation?**

A Violations can result in additional conditions, extended probation, or revocation and imprisonment.

MOVING FORWARD AFTER SENTENCING

Whether you receive probation or incarceration, your focus should shift to successful completion and moving forward.

If You Get Probation

Compliance is Everything:

- Follow all conditions exactly
- Report as required
- Pay fees on time
- Complete all requirements

Use the Opportunity:

- Address underlying issues
- Build positive relationships
- Develop job skills
- Strengthen family connections

If You're Incarcerated

Make the Most of Your Time:

- Participate in available programs
- Maintain family relationships
- Plan for release and reintegration
- Stay positive and focused on the future

Long-Term Perspective

This Isn't the End:

- Many people successfully rebuild after drug convictions
- Focus on personal growth and positive changes
- Use this experience to help others
- Remember that your past doesn't define your future

Sentencing represents a turning point in your case and your life. While facing consequences is never easy, understanding the process and preparing thoroughly can result in outcomes that allow you to rebuild and move forward. The key is demonstrating to the court that you're committed to making positive changes and contributing to your community.

In the next chapter, we'll explore what life looks like on probation and how to successfully complete community supervision in Texas.

CHAPTER 12: PROBATION AND COMMUNITY SUPERVISION

At Nancy's sentencing, the judge sentenced her to two years of community supervision - what most people call probation. Nancy felt relieved that she wasn't going to prison, but as her probation officer explained all the rules and requirements, she started to feel overwhelmed again. Monthly reporting, drug tests, community service hours, counseling sessions, and a long list of things she couldn't do. "How am I supposed to remember all of this?" she wondered.

If you've been sentenced to probation, you're probably feeling a mix of relief and anxiety right about now. Relief because you're not going to prison, but anxiety because probation comes with a lot of strings attached. The good news is that thousands of people successfully complete probation in Texas every year, including people in situations just like yours. The key is understanding that probation isn't punishment - it's an opportunity to prove you can follow the rules and stay out of trouble.

Think of your probation officer as a coach rather than a guard. Yes, they're there to make sure you follow the conditions of your supervision, but they're also there to help you succeed. Most probation officers want to see you complete the program successfully, and they've seen people overcome much bigger challenges than what you're facing. This chapter will walk you through exactly how community supervision works, what's expected of you, and most importantly, how to avoid the common mistakes that can land you in trouble. Probation might feel restrictive now, but it's your path back to a normal life.

PROBATION SUCCESS CHECKLIST

First 30 Days:

- ☐ Report to probation officer within 48 hours of sentencing
- ☐ Complete intake paperwork and assessment
- ☐ Understand all conditions of supervision
- ☐ Set up payment plan for fees and fines
- ☐ Begin any required programs or treatment
- ☐ Notify probation of current address and employment

Ongoing Requirements:

- ☐ Report as scheduled (never miss appointments)
- ☐ Pay monthly supervision fees on time
- ☐ Submit to drug testing as required
- ☐ Complete community service hours
- ☐ Attend all required classes or treatment
- ☐ Keep probation officer informed of any changes

UNDERSTANDING COMMUNITY SUPERVISION IN TEXAS

In Texas, what many people call "probation" is officially called "community supervision." Understanding the system helps you navigate it successfully.

Types of Community Supervision

Straight Probation:

- Judge finds you guilty and sentences you to probation
- Conviction is final and on your record immediately
- If you violate, punishment is limited to original sentence range
- Cannot be enhanced for future offenses

Deferred Adjudication:

- You plead guilty but judge defers finding of guilt
- No final conviction while on probation
- Successful completion will result in a no finding of guilt
- Violation can result in full punishment range
- Generally preferred by defendants

The Community Supervision Department

Who They Are:

- County employees who supervise people on probation
- Trained in case management and supervision techniques
- Required to follow state guidelines and local policies
- Accountable to judges and county commissioners

Their Dual Role:

- Help you succeed through support and resources
- Monitor compliance and report violations to court
- Balance assistance with accountability
- Connect you with community services

💡 **PROBATION PERSPECTIVE**

Your probation officer isn't your enemy - they're evaluated partly on your success. Most genuinely want to help you complete probation successfully and move forward with your life.

STANDARD CONDITIONS OF SUPERVISION

Every person on community supervision must follow certain standard conditions, regardless of their specific offense.

Basic Requirements

Report as Directed:

- Usually monthly for most offenses
- More frequent for high-risk cases
- Must report in person unless told otherwise
- Cannot miss appointments without advance permission

Pay All Financial Obligations:

- Monthly supervision fees ($60 typically)
- Court costs and fines
- Restitution to victims if applicable
- Drug testing fees

Remain in Designated Counties:

- Usually limited to county of conviction
- Some cases allow multi-county supervision
- Travel outside area requires advance permission
- Permanent moves need court approval

Avoid New Criminal Activity:

- No arrests for any offense
- Even minor violations can trigger revocation
- Traffic tickets may need to be reported
- Zero tolerance for most departments

Support Dependents:

- Continue supporting minor children
- Pay child support as ordered
- Maintain family responsibilities
- Work or actively seek employment

Employment and Education Requirements

Work Requirement:

- Maintain steady employment
- Work minimum hours (usually 30+ per week)
- Report job changes immediately
- Provide employment verification

Education Alternatives:

- Full-time students may be exempt from work requirement
- Vocational training programs often acceptable
- GED completion may be required
- Some cases require maintaining good grades

SIDEBAR: KEY TERMS

COMMUNITY SUPERVISION:

Texas's official term for probation.

SUPERVISION FEE:

Monthly payment required for probation services.

REPORTING:

Regular meetings with your probation officer.

REVOCATION:

Process of ending probation and imposing jail/prison sentence.

TECHNICAL VIOLATION:

Breaking probation rules without committing new crimes.

MODIFICATION:

Changing the conditions of your probation.

ADMINISTRATIVE CLOSURE:

Ending probation early for low-risk cases.

WARRANT:

Court order for your arrest if you violate probation.

SPECIAL CONDITIONS FOR DRUG CASES

Drug-related offenses typically include additional conditions beyond the standard requirements.

Drug Testing

Frequency:

- Random testing is most common
- May be weekly, bi-weekly, or monthly
- Frequency often decreases with good compliance
- Failed tests typically increase testing frequency

Types of Tests:

- Urinalysis (most common)
- Hair follicle testing
- Saliva testing
- Breathalyzer for alcohol

Zero Tolerance Policy:

- Any positive drug test counts as a violation
- Watered-down samples are treated as positive
- Missing a scheduled test counts as positive
- You must tell them about prescription medications with valid prescriptions

Treatment Requirements

Assessment:

- Comprehensive evaluation by licensed provider
- Determines level of care needed

- May include psychological evaluation
- Results guide treatment recommendations

Treatment Options:

- Outpatient counseling (individual and group)
- Intensive outpatient programs
- Residential treatment (if needed)
- Narcotic Anonymous/Alcoholics Anonymous meetings

Compliance Monitoring:

- Regular attendance required
- Progress reports to probation officer
- Completion certificates required
- Continued sobriety expected

Community Service

Hour Requirements:

- Typically 40-200 hours depending on offense
- Must be completed within specified timeframe
- Cannot be paid work
- Must benefit community organizations

Approved Organizations:

- Nonprofit organizations
- Government agencies
- Religious organizations
- Schools and hospitals

Documentation Required:

- Signed verification forms
- Detailed description of work performed
- Supervisor contact information
- Completion within deadlines

MONTHLY REPORTING: WHAT TO EXPECT

Your monthly meetings with your probation officer are crucial to your success.

Typical Reporting Process

Check-In Procedure:

- Arrive on time (early is better)
- Bring required documentation
- Update contact information
- Pay monthly fees

What You'll Discuss:

- Employment status and changes
- Housing situation
- Compliance with conditions
- Any problems or concerns
- Progress toward goals

What Your Officer Will Do:

- Review your compliance
- Verify employment and residence
- Schedule drug tests if required
- Address any violations
- Provide resources if needed

Information You Must Provide

Employment Updates:

- Current job status
- Hours worked
- Pay stubs or verification
- Any job changes or losses

Address Changes:

- Current residence
- Household members
- Phone numbers
- Emergency contacts

Legal Issues:

- Traffic tickets received
- Police contacts
- Court dates for other matters
- Any arrests or citations

⚠ **HONESTY IS ESSENTIAL**

Always be truthful with your probation officer. They often already know about violations before you report. Lying about problems makes everything worse and destroys the trust needed for a successful supervision.

COMMON PROBATION VIOLATIONS

Understanding what can get you in trouble helps you avoid problems.

Technical Violations

Missed Appointments:

- Failing to report as scheduled
- Not calling when unable to report
- Chronic lateness to appointments
- Missing treatment sessions

Failed Drug Tests:

- Positive tests for illegal substances
- Positive alcohol tests (if prohibited)
- Diluted or tampered samples
- Missing scheduled tests

Financial Non-Compliance:

- Not paying supervision fees
- Falling behind on court costs
- Failing to pay restitution
- Not maintaining employment

Travel Violations:

- Leaving authorized area without permission
- Failing to return from approved travel
- Moving without notification
- Extended absences

New Criminal Activity

Any New Arrests:

- Felony charges while on probation
- Misdemeanor offenses
- Traffic violations (in some cases)
- Violations in other jurisdictions

Consequences:

- Motion to revoke probation filed
- Warrant issued for arrest
- Possible return to jail pending hearing
- Risk of original sentence being imposed

VIOLATION PREVENTION STRATEGIES

Communication:

- [ ] Report problems before they become violations
- [ ] Ask for help when struggling with compliance
- [ ] Keep probation officer informed of changes
- [ ] Be proactive about potential issues

Planning:

- [ ] Set reminders for all appointments
- [ ] Budget for monthly fees and costs
- [ ] Plan transportation to meetings
- [ ] Keep backup plans for emergencies

Support Systems:

- [ ] Build relationships with positive influences
- [ ] Avoid people and places associated with drug use
- [ ] Participate in support groups
- [ ] Maintain family connections

WHAT HAPPENS IF YOU VIOLATE

If you violate probation conditions, the process that follows depends on the severity and circumstances.

The Revocation Process

Motion to Revoke:

- Probation officer reports violation to court
- Judge issues warrant for arrest
- You're taken into custody
- Revocation hearing scheduled

Burden of Proof:

- State must prove violation by preponderance of evidence
- Lower standard than "beyond reasonable doubt"
- Your probation officer will testify
- You can present evidence in your defense

Possible Outcomes:

- Warning and continue probation
- Modified conditions (more restrictive)
- Extended probation period
- Revocation and imposition of original sentence

Defending Against Revocation

Valid Defenses:

- Violation didn't actually occur
- You had permission for questioned conduct
- Emergency circumstances beyond your control
- Probation officer made errors

Mitigation Strategies:

- Show good compliance in other areas
- Demonstrate efforts to address problems
- Present evidence of positive changes
- Request modification rather than revocation

Alternatives to Revocation

Progressive Sanctions:

- Increased reporting frequency
- Additional community service hours
- Electronic monitoring
- Brief jail stays (shock probation)

Treatment Modifications:

- More intensive treatment programs
- Residential treatment requirements
- Additional counseling sessions
- Halfway house placement

SUCCESSFULLY COMPLETING PROBATION

Finishing probation successfully opens doors and provides a fresh start.

What Success Looks Like

Full Compliance:

- Perfect attendance at all appointments
- Clean drug tests throughout supervision
- All fees and costs paid in full
- Community service completed

Positive Changes:

- Stable employment or education
- Strong family relationships
- Community involvement
- Evidence of personal growth

Benefits of Successful Completion

For Straight Probation:

- Sentence completed as ordered
- No further court involvement
- Can focus on moving forward
- Demonstrates rehabilitation

For Deferred Adjudication:

- No final conviction on record
- No finding of guilt
- Eligible for non-disclosure in some cases
- Better employment and licensing prospects

Record Implications

What Stays on Your Record:

- Arrest information
- Court proceedings
- Probation supervision
- Final disposition

Sealing Options:

- Non-disclosure petitions for some deferred cases
- Expungement if charges dismissed
- Waiting periods apply
- Eligibility requirements vary

MAKING THE MOST OF YOUR OPPORTUNITY

Probation is more than just avoiding jail - it's a chance to rebuild your life.

Personal Development

Address Root Causes:

- Work on addiction issues
- Develop healthy coping skills
- Build positive relationships
- Create structure and routine

Skill Building:

- Complete education goals
- Develop job skills
- Learn financial management
- Improve communication abilities

Building Support Systems

Family Relationships:

- Rebuild trust with family members
- Take responsibility for past mistakes
- Demonstrate consistent positive changes
- Include family in recovery process

Community Connections:

- Participate in support groups
- Volunteer in community
- Build professional networks
- Develop mentor relationships

Future Planning

Career Development:

- Identify realistic career goals
- Develop necessary skills
- Build positive work history
- Plan for advancement

Personal Goals:

- Set short and long-term objectives
- Create accountability systems
- Celebrate milestones
- Focus on continuous improvement

💡 NANCY'S SUCCESS STORY

"Probation felt overwhelming at first, but my probation officer helped me see it as an opportunity. I completed my treatment, did my community service at a local clinic, and stayed clean. When I finished, I was actually grateful for the structure it gave me during a difficult time."

FREQUENTLY ASKED QUESTIONS

Q **Can I travel while on probation?**

A Local travel is usually fine, but leaving your authorized area requires advance permission from your probation officer.

Q **What happens if I lose my job while on probation?**

A Notify your probation officer immediately and show you're actively seeking new employment. Most officers work with you during brief unemployment periods.

Q **Can I get off probation early?**

A Some cases are eligible for early termination, usually after completing at least one-third of the supervision period with perfect compliance.

Q **What if I can't afford the monthly supervision fees?**

A Discuss payment plans or hardship options with your probation officer. Some departments offer community service alternatives.

Q **Can I move to another state while on probation?**

A Interstate transfers are possible but require approval from both states and meeting specific requirements.

YOUR PATH TO SUCCESS

Community supervision represents an opportunity to demonstrate that you can be a productive, law-abiding member of society. While the requirements may seem burdensome at first, they provide structure and support during a crucial transition period in your life.

Remember these keys to success:

Stay Compliant: Follow every condition exactly as ordered, no matter how minor it may seem.

Communicate: Keep your probation officer informed and ask for help when you need it.

Use Resources: Take advantage of treatment, education, and support services available.

Focus on Growth: Use this time to address underlying issues and build positive life changes.

Plan Ahead: Think about your goals for after probation and work toward them consistently.

Thousands of people successfully complete probation in Texas every year and go on to live productive, fulfilling lives. With the right attitude and commitment, you can be one of them.

In the next chapter, we'll address the immigration consequences that drug convictions can have for non-citizens, including permanent residents and those seeking citizenship.

CHAPTER 13:

IMMIGRATION

CONSEQUENCES OF DRUG CONVICTIONS

While Nancy didn't have to worry about immigration issues as a U.S. citizen, her coworker Maria - who had been arrested in a similar situation - faced an entirely different set of concerns. Maria had been living in the U.S. legally for fifteen years and was just two years away from applying for citizenship. When her attorney mentioned that a drug conviction could affect her immigration status, Maria panicked. "Could I really be deported for this?" she asked. The answer, unfortunately, was more complicated than anyone wanted it to be.

If you're not a U.S. citizen, your drug case involves much more than just criminal penalties. Immigration law has its own set of rules that don't always line up with what happens in criminal court, and what looks like a good deal from a criminal perspective might be a disaster for your immigration status. The frustrating part is that many criminal defense attorneys don't fully understand immigration consequences, so you could end up with advice that solves your criminal problem but destroys your immigration future.

Here's what you need to know: immigration law treats drug convictions very seriously, but there are often ways to structure plea agreements that minimize or avoid immigration consequences entirely. The key is making sure both your criminal attorney and an immigration lawyer are involved in your case from the beginning. This chapter will help you understand how drug convictions can affect your immigration status and what steps you need to take to protect your future in the United States.

IMMIGRATION CASE COORDINATION CHECKLIST

Immediate Steps:

- ☐ Tell your criminal attorney about your immigration status
- ☐ Consult with an immigration attorney immediately
- ☐ Gather all immigration documents
- ☐ Understand your current status and how long you've been in the U.S.
- ☐ Identify any family members who are U.S. citizens

Before Accepting Any Plea:

- ☐ Immigration attorney reviews proposed plea agreement
- ☐ Understand specific immigration consequences
- ☐ Explore alternative plea options
- ☐ Consider immigration relief options
- ☐ Document family and community ties

UNDERSTANDING IMMIGRATION STATUS CATEGORIES

Different immigration statuses face different risks from drug convictions.

Lawful Permanent Residents (Green Card Holders)

Your Current Status:

- Legal right to live and work in U.S. permanently
- Can travel internationally (with some restrictions)
- Eligible to apply for citizenship after meeting requirements
- Protected from removal except for serious crimes

Risks from Drug Convictions:

- Can trigger removal (deportation) proceedings
- May bar you from naturalization
- Could prevent re-entry if traveling abroad
- Affects ability to sponsor family members

Time in U.S. Matters:

- More than 5 years may provide some protection
- Less than 5 years creates higher deportation risk
- Continuous residence requirements for naturalization
- Longer residence may provide more relief options

Temporary Status Holders

Common Temporary Statuses:

- Work visas (H-1B, L-1, etc.)
- Student visas (F-1, M-1)

- Tourist/visitor status (B-1/B-2)
- Asylum seekers and refugees

Higher Risks:

- Easier to lose status and be removed
- Renewal applications may be denied
- Limited relief options available
- May affect future permanent residence applications

Undocumented Immigrants

Already Vulnerable Status:

- No legal right to remain in U.S.
- Subject to removal at any time
- Limited access to relief options
- Criminal convictions make removal more likely and faster

Additional Consequences:

- Bars to future legal immigration
- Affects eligibility for any relief
- May impact family members' cases
- Creates permanent inadmissibility issues

💡 **CRITICAL TIMING**

Immigration consequences attach when you're convicted, not when you're sentenced. This means deferred adjudication might not protect you, and the specific elements of your plea matter enormously.

HOW DRUG CONVICTIONS AFFECT IMMIGRATION

Immigration law treats drug offenses as particularly serious, with harsh consequences even for minor violations.

Controlled Substance Violations

What Triggers Immigration Consequences:

- Any conviction relating to controlled substances
- This includes possession, distribution, and trafficking
- Even minor possession charges can be devastating
- Marijuana offenses are treated as seriously as hard drugs

The "Reason to Believe" Standard:

- Immigration officials can act on less evidence than criminal courts
- Don't need criminal conviction in some cases
- Can use arrest records and police reports
- Admissions to officials can trigger consequences

Deportability vs. Inadmissibility

Deportability (Removal from U.S.):

- Applies to people already legally in the U.S.
- Controlled substance convictions make most non-citizens deportable
- Some exceptions for very minor marijuana possession
- Length of time in U.S. may provide relief options

Inadmissibility (Cannot Enter U.S.):

- Bars future entry or status adjustments
- Applies to almost all drug convictions
- Affects ability to get green cards or citizenship
- Travel outside U.S. can trigger inadmissibility issues

SIDEBAR: KEY TERMS

REMOVAL:

Modern term for deportation - forcing someone to leave the U.S.

DEPORTABILITY:

Legal grounds that allow removal of someone already in the U.S.

INADMISSIBILITY:

Legal bars that prevent entry or status adjustment.

AGGRAVATED FELONY:

Immigration term for serious crimes (some drug offenses qualify).

CRIME INVOLVING MORAL TURPITUDE:

Immigration category that includes many drug crimes.

CANCELLATION OF REMOVAL:

Relief that can prevent deportation in some cases.

WAIVER:

Legal forgiveness that may overcome inadmissibility.

CONSULAR PROCESSING:

Getting immigrant visas abroad (affected by drug convictions).

SPECIFIC IMMIGRATION CONSEQUENCES

For Lawful Permanent Residents

Removal Proceedings:

- Any controlled substance conviction can trigger removal
- Exception for single marijuana possession (30 grams or less)
- Multiple convictions eliminate the marijuana exception
- Delivery or sales charges always trigger removal

Naturalization Bars:

- Drug convictions can prevent citizenship applications
- May show lack of "good moral character"
- Some convictions create permanent bars
- Others require waiting periods after conviction

Travel Risks:

- Leaving U.S. can trigger inadmissibility review
- May be denied re-entry at border
- Trips over 180 days create additional risks
- Some convictions make travel extremely dangerous

For Temporary Status Holders

Status Termination:

- Current status likely to be revoked
- Removal proceedings will begin
- Future applications will be denied
- May affect family members' status

Employment Authorization:

- Work permits will be denied or revoked
- Cannot legally work in U.S.
- Employer may be required to terminate employment
- Future work authorization extremely difficult

For Asylum Seekers and Refugees

Particularly Serious Crime Bar:

- Drug trafficking convictions bar asylum
- Even minor sales charges may qualify
- No waiver available for this bar
- Can result in removal to dangerous countries

Withholding of Removal:

- Higher standard to prevent removal
- Available even when asylum is barred
- Provides protection but not path to status
- Does not allow family reunification

RELIEF OPTIONS AND WAIVERS

Despite harsh consequences, some relief may be available depending on your situation.

Cancellation of Removal for Permanent Residents

Eligibility Requirements:

- Lawful permanent resident for 5+ years
- Continuous residence for 7+ years after any admission
- Not convicted of aggravated felony

What It Provides:

- Allows you to keep green card
- Prevents removal from U.S.
- Requires immigration court proceedings
- Discretionary relief (judge decides)

Cancellation of Removal for Non-Permanent Residents

Higher Requirements:

- 10+ years continuous presence in U.S.
- Good moral character
- U.S. citizen or permanent resident family members
- Exceptional and extremely unusual hardship to family

Very Difficult to Obtain:

- Few drug cases qualify
- High burden of proof
- Discretionary relief
- Long court proceedings

Waivers of Inadmissibility

Section 212(h) Waiver:

- Available for some drug convictions
- Requires showing extreme hardship to U.S. citizen family
- Not available for drug trafficking
- Complex application process

Other Waiver Options:

- Limited availability for drug convictions
- Strict eligibility requirements
- Expensive and time-consuming
- No guarantee of approval

⚠️ **PLEA BARGAIN CAUTION**

What seems like a great criminal plea deal might be terrible for immigration. A misdemeanor plea that avoids jail time could still trigger deportation. Always get immigration advice before accepting any plea.

WORKING WITH IMMIGRATION AND CRIMINAL ATTORNEYS

Managing both criminal and immigration cases requires coordination between attorneys.

Why You Need Both

Criminal Attorney's Role:

- Negotiates plea agreements
- Understands criminal law and procedure
- Focuses on avoiding criminal penalties
- May not understand immigration consequences

Immigration Attorney's Role:

- Understands immigration law consequences
- Knows which pleas trigger problems
- Can suggest plea alternatives
- Handles removal defense if needed

Coordination is Essential:

- Immigration attorney reviews all plea offers
- Criminal attorney modifies negotiations based on immigration advice
- Both work together on timing and strategy
- Client makes informed decisions with full information

Questions for Your Criminal Attorney

Immigration Awareness:

- Do you regularly handle cases for non-citizens?
- Will you consult with immigration attorney before advising on pleas?
- Do you understand the difference between deportability and inadmissibility?
- Have you handled similar cases with immigration issues?

Questions for Your Immigration Attorney

Criminal Case Experience:

- Do you regularly work with criminal defense attorneys?
- Can you review plea offers quickly?
- Do you handle removal defense?
- What relief options might be available in my case?

PLEA NEGOTIATION STRATEGIES

Immigration-Safe Plea Options:

- ☐ Charges that don't involve controlled substances
- ☐ Dispositions that avoid "conviction" for immigration purposes
- ☐ Pleas to crimes that don't trigger mandatory removal
- ☐ Sentences that preserve relief eligibility

Pleas to Avoid:

- ☐ Any controlled substance offense
- ☐ Aggravated felony charges
- ☐ Crimes involving moral turpitude
- ☐ Multiple convictions of any kind

Timing Considerations:

- ☐ Apply for naturalization before plea if eligible
- ☐ Consider effect on pending applications
- ☐ Understand travel restrictions after conviction
- ☐ Plan for potential removal proceedings

SPECIAL CONSIDERATIONS FOR DIFFERENT SITUATIONS

Applying for Naturalization

Current Applications:

- Withdraw application before plea if possible
- Drug convictions can result in denial
- Failed naturalization can trigger removal proceedings
- May be better to delay until after criminal case

Future Applications:

- Some convictions create permanent bars
- Others require waiting periods
- Good moral character requirements
- May need waivers for inadmissibility

Family Members in Immigration Process

Sponsorship Issues:

- Drug convictions may affect ability to sponsor family
- Pending family cases may be affected
- Consider impact on spouse and children's cases
- Some family members may lose status

Protective Measures:

- File family applications before plea if possible
- Consider separate representation for family members
- Understand derivative consequences
- Plan for potential family separation

Employment-Based Status

Current Employment:

- Employer may terminate after conviction
- Security clearances likely to be revoked
- Professional licenses affected
- Future employment opportunities limited

Status Consequences:

- Work authorization revoked
- Future visa applications denied
- Employer sponsorship unlikely
- Return to home country may be necessary

IF REMOVAL PROCEEDINGS BEGIN

If you're placed in removal proceedings, you need specialized legal help immediately.

The Removal Process

Notice to Appear:

- Formal charging document from immigration court
- Lists charges and factual allegations
- Sets initial hearing date
- Begins formal removal proceedings

Master Calendar Hearing:

- Initial court appearance
- Admit or deny charges
- Declare what relief you're seeking
- Get deadlines for applications

Individual Hearing:

- Trial on your applications for relief
- Present evidence and witnesses
- Government argues for removal
- Judge decides your case

Preparing Your Defense

Gathering Evidence:

- Family relationships and ties
- Community involvement
- Employment history
- Rehabilitation efforts

Witness Testimony:

- Family members
- Community leaders
- Employers
- Treatment providers

Legal Arguments:

- Challenge removability charges
- Apply for all available relief
- Argue for prosecutorial discretion
- Seek voluntary departure if necessary

PROTECTING YOUR FUTURE

Even with a drug conviction, you may have options to protect your immigration status.

Immediate Protective Steps

Document Everything:

- Keep records of all time in U.S.
- Gather evidence of family relationships
- Document community ties and employment
- Collect character references

Stay in Status:

- Comply with all immigration requirements
- Don't overstay any authorized period
- Keep all documents current
- Avoid any additional criminal activity

Long-Term Planning

Rehabilitation Evidence:

- Complete treatment programs
- Maintain steady employment
- Participate in community activities
- Build strong family relationships

Legal Options:

- Monitor changes in immigration law
- Consider future waiver applications
- Explore family-based relief options
- Plan for potential relief legislation

MARIA'S OUTCOME

"My criminal attorney worked with an immigration lawyer to structure a plea that avoided immigration consequences. It took longer to negotiate, but I kept my green card and became a citizen two years later. The coordination between attorneys saved my American dream."

FREQUENTLY ASKED QUESTIONS

Q **Will deferred adjudication protect me from immigration consequences?**

A Not necessarily. Immigration law has its own definition of «conviction» that may include deferred adjudication.

Q **Can I travel outside the U.S. with a drug conviction?**

A It's very risky. You may be denied re-entry, especially with permanent resident status.

Q **What if I'm already a U.S. citizen?**

A Citizens cannot be deported, but naturalization obtained through fraud can be revoked.

Q **Should I self-deport to avoid proceedings?**

A This is a major decision that requires careful consultation with an immigration attorney.

Q **Can my family members be affected by my conviction?**

A Yes, your conviction can impact family members' immigration cases and applications.

PROTECTING YOUR AMERICAN DREAM

Drug charges are serious for everyone, but for non-citizens, they can threaten your entire future in the United States. The key to protecting yourself is understanding the risks and working with attorneys who understand both criminal and immigration law.

Remember these crucial points:

Get Immigration Advice Early: Don't wait until after your criminal case is resolved.

Coordinate Your Defense: Make sure your criminal and immigration attorneys work together.

Understand All Consequences: What helps your criminal case might hurt your immigration status.

Explore All Options: There may be relief available even with serious charges.

Plan for the Future: Consider long-term immigration goals in your immediate decisions.

Your immigration status is too important to leave to chance. With proper legal guidance and strategic planning, you may be able to resolve your criminal case while protecting your right to remain in the United States.

In the next chapter, we'll examine how drug convictions can affect professional licenses and what steps you can take to protect your career.

CHAPTER 14: PROFESSIONAL LICENSE IMPACTS

From the moment Nancy was arrested, her biggest fear wasn't jail time or fines - it was losing her nursing license. She'd worked hard to build her career, and the thought of being banned from the profession she loved was devastating. "Will I ever be able to work as a nurse again?" she asked her attorney during their first meeting. The answer wasn't simple, but it wasn't hopeless either. Professional licensing boards have their own rules and procedures, and understanding how they work can make all the difference in protecting your career.

If you hold a professional license - whether you're a nurse like Nancy, a teacher, real estate agent, doctor, lawyer, or any other licensed professional - you're probably terrified about what your drug charge means for your livelihood. The reality is that licensing boards take drug convictions seriously, but they're not automatically career-killers. Each profession has different standards, and many boards focus more on rehabilitation and current fitness to practice than on past mistakes.

The key to protecting your license is understanding that you're actually dealing with two separate processes: your criminal case and your licensing board investigation. These don't always happen at the same time, and what you do in your criminal case can significantly impact what happens with your license. This chapter will walk you through how licensing boards operate, what triggers their attention, and most importantly, how to position yourself for the best possible outcome in both arenas. Your career isn't necessarily over - you just need to handle things strategically.

PROFESSIONAL LICENSE PROTECTION CHECKLIST

Immediate Actions:

- ☐ Review your licensing board's rules about criminal charges
- ☐ Determine reporting requirements and deadlines
- ☐ Gather all professional history documentation
- ☐ Contact a professional license defense attorney
- ☐ Consider voluntary treatment or rehabilitation programs

During Criminal Case:

- ☐ Coordinate criminal and license defense strategies
- ☐ Keep detailed records of all rehabilitation efforts
- ☐ Maintain professional conduct and continuing education
- ☐ Document community support and character references
- ☐ Prepare for potential license board investigation

UNDERSTANDING PROFESSIONAL LICENSING BOARDS

Professional licensing boards exist to protect the public by ensuring that licensed professionals meet standards of competence and character.

How Licensing Boards Operate

Regulatory Function:

- Set standards for entry into professions
- Monitor ongoing fitness to practice
- Investigate complaints and violations
- Impose discipline when necessary
- Protect public safety and welfare

Separate from Criminal Courts:

- Independent investigation and hearing process
- Different standards of evidence
- Focus on professional fitness rather than punishment
- Administrative rather than criminal proceedings

Board Composition:

- Practicing professionals in the field
- Public members representing consumers
- Appointed by state officials
- Volunteers serving fixed terms

Common Types of Professional Licenses

Healthcare Professions:

- Nurses (RN, LVN, NP)

- Doctors and physicians
- Dentists and dental hygienists
- Pharmacists and pharmacy technicians
- Physical therapists and occupational therapists

Legal and Financial:

- Attorneys
- Certified Public Accountants
- Insurance agents
- Real estate agents and brokers
- Financial advisors

Education and Public Safety:

- Teachers and school administrators
- Law enforcement officers
- Security guards
- Social workers
- Mental health counselors

Skilled Trades:

- Contractors and electricians
- Plumbers and HVAC technicians
- Cosmetologists and barbers
- Massage therapists
- Commercial drivers

DUAL TRACK REALITY

Your criminal case and license investigation are separate proceedings with different rules, timelines, and potential outcomes. Success in one doesn't guarantee success in the other, but failure in one doesn't doom the other either.

HOW DRUG CHARGES TRIGGER LICENSE ACTIONS

Understanding what catches licensing boards' attention helps you prepare for potential investigations.

Reporting Requirements

Self-Reporting Obligations:

- Most licenses require reporting arrests within specific time-frames
- Some require reporting only convictions
- Failure to report can result in additional consequences
- Deadlines are strict and missing them makes things worse

Automatic Notifications:

- Some boards receive automatic reports from criminal courts
- Background check companies may report arrests
- Professional associations sometimes notify boards
- Employers may report employee arrests

Timing Variations:

- Some boards want immediate notification
- Others require reporting within 30-90 days
- Conviction reporting deadlines may be different from arrest reporting
- Check your specific board's rules carefully

What Triggers Investigations

Arrest Reports:

- Even without conviction, arrest may trigger investigation
- Boards concerned about public safety and professional image
- Nature of charges influences board response
- Drug charges are particularly concerning to most boards

Conviction Records:

- Any conviction typically triggers formal investigation
- Deferred adjudication may or may not count as conviction
- Plea agreements don't eliminate licensing consequences
- Multiple convictions create cumulative concerns

Related Professional Issues:

- Practicing under the influence
- Theft of drugs from workplace
- Prescription fraud or diversion
- Patient safety concerns

SIDEBAR: KEY TERMS

PROFESSIONAL LICENSE:

State-issued authorization to practice a specific profession.

LICENSING BOARD:

State agency that regulates specific professions.

DISCIPLINARY ACTION:

Formal sanctions imposed by licensing boards.

FITNESS TO PRACTICE:

Standard for determining whether someone should hold a license.

SELF-REPORTING:

Requirement to notify licensing board of arrests or convictions.

CONSENT AGREEMENT:

Settlement between licensee and board avoiding formal hearing.

PROBATIONARY LICENSE:

Restricted license allowing practice under supervision.

SUMMARY SUSPENSION:

Emergency removal of license pending investigation.

TYPES OF DISCIPLINARY ACTIONS

Licensing boards have various tools for addressing professional misconduct.

Minor Sanctions

Reprimand or Censure:

- Formal criticism placed in license file
- Usually public record
- Minimal impact on practice
- Often combined with other sanctions

Continuing Education Requirements:

- Additional training beyond normal requirements
- Ethics courses common for drug-related violations
- Substance abuse education
- Professional development programs

Fines and Administrative Costs:

- Monetary penalties for violations
- Reimbursement of investigation costs
- Payment plans usually available
- Amount varies by profession and violation

Moderate Sanctions

Probationary License:

- Allows continued practice under restrictions
- Regular monitoring and reporting required
- May include practice limitations
- Violation can result in suspension

Practice Restrictions:

- Limited scope of practice
- Supervision requirements
- Workplace monitoring
- Specific prohibited activities

Substance Abuse Monitoring:

- Regular drug testing
- Participation in recovery programs
- Treatment compliance requirements
- Monitoring by board-approved programs

Severe Sanctions

License Suspension:

- Temporary prohibition from practice
- Can range from months to years
- Reinstatement requires meeting specific conditions
- Income and career impact significant

License Revocation:

- Permanent loss of license
- Most severe sanction available
- May be eligible for reapplication after years
- Extremely difficult to overcome

Summary Suspension:

- Emergency removal for immediate public danger
- Pending full investigation and hearing
- Used when continued practice poses risk
- Can be devastating professionally and financially

LICENSE-SPECIFIC CONSIDERATIONS

Different professions have varying approaches to drug-related violations.

Healthcare Licenses

Nursing Boards:

- Very concerned about drug abuse due to patient safety
- Access to controlled substances in workplace
- Alternative-to-discipline programs often available
- Focus on treatment and monitoring rather than punishment

Medical Licenses:

- Prescribing authority makes drug issues serious
- Emphasis on rehabilitation and monitoring
- Physician health programs in most states
- Return to practice possible with proper treatment

Pharmacy Licenses:

- Direct access to controlled substances
- Theft or diversion extremely serious
- Background checks for all pharmacy employees
- Substance abuse programs specifically designed for pharmacists

Legal Licenses

Attorney Licenses:

- Drug convictions often result in suspension
- Moral character requirements very strict
- Treatment and rehabilitation heavily weighted

- Client trust and professional image paramount

Law Enforcement:

- Zero tolerance policies common
- Criminal conviction often means automatic termination
- Credibility as witness in court compromised
- Appeals process usually internal to department

Education Licenses

Teacher Certifications:

- Student safety primary concern
- Moral character requirements strict
- Media attention can influence board decisions
- Alternative certification paths may be available

Administrative Positions:

- Higher standards for leadership roles
- Budget and personnel responsibilities
- Community trust and image important
- Professional development often required

⚠ TIMING STRATEGY

When you report to your licensing board can significantly impact the outcome. Reporting immediately after arrest shows honesty but may trigger premature action. Waiting until conviction avoids multiple proceedings but may look like hiding something.

BUILDING YOUR DEFENSE STRATEGY

Protecting your professional license requires a strategic approach that coordinates with your criminal defense.

Early Intervention

Voluntary Treatment:

- Enroll in treatment before being required
- Shows recognition of problem and commitment to change
- Demonstrates proactive approach to rehabilitation
- May influence both criminal and licensing outcomes

Professional Development:

- Continue education and training
- Maintain professional associations
- Participate in professional activities
- Show ongoing commitment to profession

Character References:

- Colleagues and supervisors
- Patients or clients (if appropriate)
- Professional mentors
- Community leaders

Documentation Strategy

Rehabilitation Evidence:

- Treatment program completion certificates
- Sponsor statements from recovery programs
- Counseling records (with proper releases)
- Drug testing results showing sobriety

Professional Competence:

- Performance evaluations
- Continuing education transcripts
- Professional awards and recognition
- Patient satisfaction surveys

Community Support:

- Character reference letters
- Community service documentation
- Religious or organizational involvement
- Volunteer work records

LICENSE DEFENSE PREPARATION

Gather Professional Records:

- ☐ Complete employment history
- ☐ Performance evaluations and reviews
- ☐ Professional development and training records
- ☐ Any previous board interactions
- ☐ Professional liability insurance claims history

Document Rehabilitation:

- ☐ Treatment program enrollment and completion
- ☐ Counseling records and progress notes
- ☐ Sponsor statements from recovery programs
- ☐ Drug testing records showing sobriety
- ☐ Continuing education beyond requirements

Character Evidence:

- ☐ Letters from colleagues and supervisors
- ☐ Patient or client testimonials (where appropriate)
- ☐ Community service documentation
- ☐ Professional association involvement
- ☐ Awards and recognition

WORKING WITH PROFESSIONAL LICENSE ATTORNEYS

Professional license defense requires specialized knowledge and experience.

Why You Need Specialized Counsel

Different Legal Standards:

- Administrative law rather than criminal law
- Preponderance of evidence standard
- Professional fitness rather than guilt/innocence
- Regulatory rather than constitutional focus

Board-Specific Experience:

- Knowledge of specific board procedures
- Relationships with board members and staff
- Understanding of informal resolution options
- Experience with professional rehabilitation programs

Coordination with Criminal Case:

- Timing strategy for reporting and proceedings
- Plea agreement implications for licensing
- Evidence sharing between cases
- Witness coordination

Experience Questions:

- How many cases have you handled before this specific board?
- What's your success rate with drug-related violations?
- Do you work with criminal attorneys on coordinated defense?
- Can you provide references from other professionals?

Strategy Questions:

- Should I report immediately or wait for conviction?
- What rehabilitation steps should I take now?
- Are there alternative-to-discipline programs available?
- What's the realistic range of potential outcomes?

ALTERNATIVE-TO-DISCIPLINE PROGRAMS

Many licensing boards offer rehabilitation-focused alternatives to traditional discipline.

Professional Health Programs

How They Work:

- Voluntary participation (usually)
- Focus on treatment and monitoring
- Confidential or private process
- Successful completion avoids public discipline

Common Features:

- Comprehensive evaluation and treatment
- Regular drug testing and monitoring
- Practice restrictions or supervision
- Peer support and mentoring

Benefits:

- Avoid public discipline
- Keep license and continue practicing
- Focus on health rather than punishment
- Better long-term career prospects

Consent Agreements

Negotiated Settlements:

- Agreement between licensee and board
- Avoids formal hearing process
- Specific terms tailored to situation
- Public record but less severe than formal discipline

Common Terms:

- Probationary license period
- Treatment and monitoring requirements
- Practice restrictions or supervision
- Continuing education requirements

Conditional Licenses

Restricted Practice:

- Allows practice under specific conditions
- Workplace monitoring
- Limited scope of practice
- Regular reporting requirements

Reinstatement Path:

- Clear requirements for full license restoration
- Demonstration of rehabilitation
- Period of successful compliance
- Professional competence evaluation

PREPARING FOR BOARD HEARINGS

If your case goes to a formal hearing, thorough preparation is essential.

The Hearing Process

Pre-Hearing Preparation:

- Discovery of board's evidence
- Witness preparation and coordination
- Exhibit preparation and organization
- Strategy development with counsel

Hearing Procedures:

- Administrative law judge or board panel
- Rules of evidence less strict than criminal court
- Both sides present evidence and witnesses
- Decision based on preponderance of evidence

Post-Hearing Process:

- Written decision with findings
- Appeal rights to state courts
- Implementation of sanctions
- Compliance monitoring

Testifying at Your Hearing

Preparation is Key:

- Review all facts and timeline
- Practice with your attorney
- Understand likely questions
- Prepare for cross-examination

Key Messages:

- Accept responsibility for actions
- Demonstrate understanding of impact
- Show commitment to rehabilitation
- Emphasize fitness to practice

What to Avoid:

- Minimizing the seriousness
- Blaming others
- Being defensive or angry
- Showing lack of insight

💡 **NANCY'S LICENSE OUTCOME**

"My nursing board placed me on probationary status for two years with quarterly reporting and random drug testing. It was stressful, but I kept my license and continued working. The board saw that I was serious about recovery and completing my criminal probation successfully. After two years, my license was fully restored."

LONG-TERM CAREER MANAGEMENT

Even with successful license defense, managing your professional reputation requires ongoing attention.

Rebuilding Professional Standing

Consistent Performance:

- Exceed expectations in your work
- Volunteer for additional responsibilities
- Maintain perfect compliance with any restrictions
- Seek leadership opportunities when appropriate

Professional Development:

- Continue education beyond requirements
- Obtain additional certifications
- Participate in professional organizations
- Mentor others in your field

Community Involvement:

- Volunteer in community organizations
- Participate in professional service
- Speak about recovery if appropriate
- Give back to your profession

Managing Disclosure

Employment Applications:

- Understand what must be disclosed
- Focus on rehabilitation and growth
- Be prepared to explain circumstances
- Provide context and current status

Professional Relationships:

- Be selective about disclosure
- Focus on current competence
- Let work performance speak for itself
- Address concerns directly if raised

Future Opportunities

Career Advancement:

- May face initial limitations
- Demonstrate exceptional performance
- Build strong reputation for reliability
- Consider areas where experience adds value

Helping Others:

- Recovery experience can be valuable
- Mentoring colleagues with similar issues
- Advocacy for better professional support
- Speaking about lessons learned

FREQUENTLY ASKED QUESTIONS

Q **Do I have to report an arrest even if charges are later dismissed?**

A It depends on your specific licensing board's rules. Some require reporting arrests, others only convictions. Check your board's requirements carefully.

Q **Can I practice while my license case is pending?**

A Usually yes, unless the board imposes an emergency suspension. However, some employers may suspend you pending resolution.

Q **Will my malpractice insurance cover license defense costs?**

A Some policies include administrative proceeding coverage, but many don't. Check your policy and consider separate coverage.

Q **Can I get a license in another state if I lose mine in Texas?**

A Other states will know about Texas discipline and may deny licensure. However, some states consider rehabilitation evidence.

Q **How long do license disciplinary actions stay on my record?**

A Usually permanently, though some states allow removal after many years of good standing.

PROTECTING YOUR PROFESSIONAL FUTURE

Your professional license represents years of education, training, and investment in your career. While drug charges pose serious risks to your license, they don't necessarily mean the end of your professional life.

Key strategies for protecting your license:

Act Quickly: Get specialized legal help immediately and understand your reporting obligations.

Coordinate Defense: Make sure your criminal and license attorneys work together on strategy.

Demonstrate Rehabilitation: Take proactive steps to address underlying issues and show commitment to change.

Document Everything: Keep detailed records of all rehabilitation efforts and professional activities.

Stay Engaged: Continue participating in your profession and community while cases are pending.

Plan Long-Term: Consider how current decisions affect your entire career trajectory.

With proper planning and representation, many professionals successfully navigate drug charges while preserving their careers. The key is taking the right steps early and maintaining focus on both legal defense and professional rehabilitation.

In the next chapter, we'll examine the appeals process and your options if you're convicted and believe errors were made during your trial.

CHAPTER 15:

APPEALS PROCESS

DON'T STRESS ABOUT THIS YET

Appeals are only necessary if you're convicted and believe legal errors occurred. If you're early in your case, focus on building the strongest possible defense first. Most people never need to appeal because their cases are resolved favorably before trial.

If you've been convicted and believe errors were made during your trial, the appeals process gives you a powerful tool to challenge that conviction. Appeals courts exist specifically to review trial court decisions and correct legal mistakes, and they overturn convictions more often than you might think. This isn't about getting a second bite at the apple or re-arguing the facts of your case - it's about holding trial courts accountable for following the law correctly.

You have the right to appeal your conviction, and appellate courts take that right seriously. When trial judges make legal errors, when prosecutors engage in misconduct, or when defense attorneys provide ineffective assistance, appeals courts have the authority and responsibility to fix those problems. The appellate process follows strict rules and deadlines, but if you have legitimate grounds for appeal, this could be your path to a better outcome. This chapter will show you exactly how appeals work, what issues can be successfully challenged, and how to position your case for the best chance of success. Your conviction doesn't have to be the final word on your case.

APPEALS TIMELINE CHECKLIST

Critical Deadlines:

- ☐ File notice of appeal within 30 days of sentencing
- ☐ Request court reporter's record within 30 days
- ☐ Pay appellate costs or file affidavit of indigency
- ☐ Consider appeal bond if seeking to remain free during appeal
- ☐

Appeal Process Steps:

- ☐ Notice of appeal filed with trial court
- ☐ Record prepared and transmitted to appellate court
- ☐ Appellant's brief filed (usually within 30-60 days of record filing)
- ☐ State's brief filed in response
- ☐ Oral argument scheduled (if requested and granted)
- ☐ Court issues written decision

UNDERSTANDING THE APPEALS PROCESS

Appeals are fundamentally different from trials, focusing on legal issues rather than factual disputes.

What Appeals Courts Do

Review Legal Errors:

- Examine whether trial court followed proper legal procedures
- Determine if evidence was properly admitted or excluded
- Review jury instructions for legal accuracy
- Evaluate whether constitutional rights were protected

What They Don't Do:

- Re-examine witness credibility
- Reweigh evidence
- Decide guilt or innocence based on facts
- Consider new evidence not presented at trial

Types of Appellate Courts in Texas

Courts of Appeals:

- Intermediate appellate courts
- Handle most criminal appeals
- Review trial court decisions
- Issue written opinions

Texas Court of Criminal Appeals:

- Highest criminal court in Texas
- Reviews death penalty cases automatically
- Discretionary review of other cases
- Final authority on state criminal law

Federal Courts:

- Available for constitutional issues
- Habeas corpus proceedings
- Very limited circumstances
- Usually after state appeals exhausted

💡 **APPEALS REALITY CHECK**

Appeals courts assume the trial court got it right and look for clear errors. The burden is on you to show that mistakes were made and that those mistakes affected the outcome of your case.

GROUNDS FOR APPEAL IN DRUG CASES

Not every trial error justifies overturning a conviction. Appeals courts focus on significant legal mistakes.

Constitutional Violations

Fourth Amendment Issues:

- Illegal searches and seizures
- Evidence obtained without warrants
- Searches exceeding scope of consent
- Violations of Miranda rights

Fifth Amendment Problems:

- Forced self-incrimination
- Double jeopardy violations
- Due process violations
- Coerced confessions

Sixth Amendment Violations:

- Ineffective assistance of counsel
- Denial of right to confront witnesses
- Denial of right to jury trial
- Inadequate legal representation

Evidence Problems

Improperly Admitted Evidence:

- Evidence that should have been suppressed
- Hearsay evidence admitted without proper foundation
- Character evidence improperly allowed
- Prejudicial evidence that outweighed probative value

Improperly Excluded Evidence:

- Defense evidence wrongly kept from jury
- Witness testimony improperly limited
- Expert testimony incorrectly excluded
- Constitutional right to present defense violated

Trial Court Errors

Incorrect Jury Instructions:

- Wrong statements of law
- Confusing or contradictory instructions
- Failure to instruct on lesser included offenses
- Instructions that shifted burden of proof

Prosecutorial Misconduct:

- Improper closing arguments
- Withholding exculpatory evidence
- Improper witness coaching
- Inflammatory or prejudicial statements

Judicial Errors:

- Abuse of discretion in evidentiary rulings
- Improper communications with jury
- Bias or prejudice shown by judge
- Incorrect application of sentencing law

SIDEBAR: KEY TERMS

NOTICE OF APPEAL:

Document filed to begin the appellate process.

RECORD ON APPEAL:

Complete transcript and documents from trial court.

APPELLANT:

Person filing the appeal (you).

APPELLEE:

Responding party (the state).

BRIEF:

Written legal argument submitted to appellate court.

SIDEBAR: KEY TERMS

HARMLESS ERROR:

A mistake that didn't change the outcome. For example, if the judge let in evidence that shouldn't have been allowed, but there was so much other evidence that you would have been convicted anyway, the appeals court won't overturn your case.

REVERSIBLE ERROR:

A serious mistake that probably changed the outcome. For example, if the judge gave wrong jury instructions about what the state had to prove, and this confusion may have led to your conviction.

REMAND:

Sending case back to trial court for further proceedings.

THE APPEALS PROCESS STEP BY STEP

Understanding each stage helps you know what to expect during your appeal.

Filing the Notice of Appeal

Critical 30-Day Deadline:

- Must be filed within 30 days of sentencing
- No extensions available
- Missing deadline usually ends appeal rights
- Filed with trial court clerk

What the Notice Includes:

- Your name and cause number
- Judgment being appealed
- Court to which appeal is taken
- Signature of defendant or attorney

Costs and Fees:

- Filing fees required
- Court reporter costs
- Appellate record preparation fees
- May file affidavit of indigency if you can't afford costs

Preparing the Record

Court Reporter's Transcript:

- Complete record of all trial proceedings
- Must be requested within 30 days
- Expensive but essential for appeal
- Can request only portions to save money

Clerk's Record:

- All documents filed in trial court
- Exhibits admitted at trial
- Jury instructions and verdict
- Sentencing documents

Record Transmission:

- Trial court sends complete record to appellate court
- Usually takes 60-120 days
- Appeal officially begins when record filed
- Clock starts for briefing schedule

Brief Writing

Appellant's Brief (Your Brief):

- Legal arguments for overturning conviction
- Citations to record and legal authorities
- Clear statement of errors claimed
- Request for specific relief

State's Brief:

- Response defending trial court's decisions
- Arguments that any errors were harmless
- Citations supporting conviction
- Request to affirm conviction

Reply Brief (Optional):

- Your response to state's arguments
- Cannot raise new issues
- Limited to responding to state's brief
- Opportunity to clarify arguments

INEFFECTIVE ASSISTANCE OF COUNSEL CLAIMS

One of the most common grounds for appeal in drug cases involves inadequate legal representation.

Standards for Ineffective Assistance

Deficient Performance:

- Attorney's representation fell below objective standard
- Made errors that reasonable attorney wouldn't make
- Failed to investigate obvious defenses
- Lacked basic knowledge of criminal law

Prejudice to Defense:

- Errors actually affected outcome of case
- Reasonable probability result would have been different
- Not enough to show attorney made mistakes
- Must show mistakes mattered to verdict

Common Examples in Drug Cases

Failure to File Suppression Motions:

- Obvious Fourth Amendment violations ignored
- Search and seizure issues not challenged
- Statements taken in violation of Miranda
- Chain of custody problems not addressed

Inadequate Investigation:

- Failed to interview witnesses
- Didn't consult with experts
- Ignored obvious defenses
- Rushed through case preparation

Conflict of Interest:

- Representing co-defendants with conflicting interests
- Financial conflicts affecting representation
- Personal relationships affecting judgment
- Prior attorney-client relationships creating problems

Developing Ineffective Assistance Claims

Documenting Deficiencies:

- Identify specific acts or omissions
- Show what reasonable attorney would have done
- Gather evidence of inadequate preparation
- Interview witnesses attorney should have called

Proving Prejudice:

- Show how different representation would have changed outcome
- Demonstrate that errors affected jury verdict
- Prove that better investigation would have revealed helpful evidence
- Establish that proper legal arguments would have succeeded

⚠ APPEAL BOND CONSIDERATION

You'll usually remain in custody during your appeal unless you post an appeal bond. Appeal bonds are expensive and require strong appellate issues. Most people serve their sentences while appeals are pending.

WHAT HAPPENS IF YOU WIN YOUR APPEAL

Winning an appeal doesn't always mean you're free - it depends on what the appellate court finds.

Possible Outcomes

Reversal and Dismissal:

- Conviction overturned completely
- Charges dismissed
- Cannot be retried
- Complete victory

Reversal and Remand for New Trial:

- Conviction overturned
- Case sent back for new trial
- State can retry you
- Second chance at better outcome

Reversal of Sentence Only:

- Conviction stands
- Sentence overturned for legal errors
- New sentencing hearing required
- Opportunity for better sentence

Modification of Conviction:

- Conviction reduced to lesser offense
- Some charges dismissed
- Sentence may be reduced accordingly
- Partial victory

Preparing for Retrial

If Granted New Trial:

- State decides whether to retry case
- Same charges or reduced charges possible
- Different attorney may be needed
- Lessons learned from first trial apply

Strategic Considerations:

- Why did first trial go wrong?
- What evidence might be excluded on retrial?
- Are there plea negotiations possible?
- Has state's case gotten weaker over time?

APPEAL EVALUATION CHECKLIST

Strength of Appellate Issues:

- [ ] Clear legal errors occurred during trial
- [ ] Errors likely affected the outcome
- [ ] Strong legal precedent supports your position
- [ ] Record clearly shows the problems

Practical Considerations:

- [ ] Cost of appeal vs. potential benefits
- [ ] Time remaining on sentence
- [ ] Likelihood of success
- [ ] Impact on family and employment

Alternative Options:

- [ ] Habeas corpus petition
- [ ] Motion for new trial
- [ ] Plea negotiations with state
- [ ] Focus on early parole or release

HABEAS CORPUS PROCEEDINGS

Sometimes issues arise that can't be addressed through regular appeals.

What Habeas Corpus Covers

Issues Not Raised at Trial:

- Newly discovered evidence
- Constitutional violations not apparent during trial
- Ineffective assistance of counsel
- Prosecutorial misconduct discovered later

When Available:

- After direct appeal completed or waived
- When fundamental rights violated
- For claims requiring evidence outside trial record
- Time limits vary by type of claim

State vs. Federal Habeas

State Habeas Corpus:

- Filed in Texas courts
- Broader range of claims available
- More flexible procedural rules
- Must usually be filed before federal habeas

Federal Habeas Corpus:

- Filed in federal district court
- Limited to federal constitutional violations
- Strict procedural requirements
- Usually requires exhausting state remedies first

SELECTING APPEAL COUNSEL

Appeals require specialized knowledge and skills different from trial work.

Appellate vs. Trial Attorneys

Different Skill Sets:

- Appellate attorneys focus on legal research and writing
- Trial attorneys focus on jury persuasion and courtroom advocacy
- Appeals require deep knowledge of procedural rules
- Different strategic thinking required

Why Specialization Matters:

- Appellate courts have unique procedures
- Brief writing is specialized skill
- Oral argument techniques differ from trial advocacy
- Relationships with appellate court staff helpful

Questions for Potential Appeal Counsel

Experience Questions:

- How many criminal appeals have you handled?
- What's your success rate in drug cases?
- Do you regularly practice before this appellate court?
- Can you provide references from other clients?

Strategy Questions:

- What appellate issues do you see in my case?
- What are my realistic chances of success?
- How long will the appeal process take?
- What are the total costs involved?

Communication Questions:

- How often will you update me on progress?
- Will you handle oral argument personally?
- How do you prepare clients for the appeals process?
- What's your timeline for filing briefs?

MANAGING EXPECTATIONS

Appeals are challenging, and understanding realistic outcomes helps you make informed decisions.

Success Rates

Overall Statistics:

- Most criminal appeals are unsuccessful
- Drug cases have moderate success rates
- Constitutional violations more likely to succeed
- Evidentiary issues harder to win

Factors Affecting Success:

- Strength of legal issues
- Quality of trial record
- Skill of appellate counsel
- Specific appellate court tendencies

Time and Cost Considerations

Appeal Timeline:

- Usually takes 12-24 months
- Complex cases may take longer
- Expedited appeals rare in drug cases
- Court backlogs affect timing

Financial Costs:

- Attorney fees for appellate counsel
- Court costs and filing fees
- Record preparation expenses
- Appeal bond costs if seeking release

Alternative Strategies

Focus on Sentence Completion:

- Concentrate on early parole
- Participate in prison programs
- Build record for commutation
- Plan for successful reentry

Collateral Relief:

- Challenge conviction in other proceedings
- Seek record sealing or expungement
- Focus on professional license restoration
- Address immigration consequences

FREQUENTLY ASKED QUESTIONS

Q How long do I have to file an appeal?

A You must file a notice of appeal within 30 days of sentencing. This deadline is absolute and cannot be extended.

Q Can I remain free during my appeal?

A Only if you post an appeal bond, which is expensive and requires strong appellate issues. Most people serve their sentences during appeals.

Q What if I can't afford an appellate attorney?

A You may be entitled to appointed counsel for your first appeal. Apply with the appellate court or through your trial attorney.

Q Can new evidence be considered on appeal?

A Generally no. Appeals are limited to the record made at trial. New evidence usually requires habeas corpus proceedings.

Q What happens if I win my appeal?

A Depends on the ruling. You might get a new trial, have charges dismissed, or get a new sentencing hearing.

MAKING THE APPEAL DECISION

Deciding whether to appeal requires careful analysis of legal, practical, and personal factors.

Consider Appeals When:

- ☐ Clear legal errors occurred during trial
- ☐ Constitutional rights were violated
- ☐ Attorney provided ineffective assistance
- ☐ Sentence is severe enough to justify costs and delay

Consider Alternatives When:

- ☐ Appellate issues are weak
- ☐ Sentence is relatively light
- ☐ Costs outweigh potential benefits
- ☐ You want to move forward with your life

Key Factors to Evaluate:

- ☐ Strength of appellate issues
- ☐ Likelihood of success
- ☐ Cost vs. benefit analysis
- ☐ Impact on family and future plans
- ☐ Time remaining on sentence

Remember, appeals are about correcting legal errors, not relitigating your guilt or innocence. If you have strong appellate issues and the resources to pursue them, appeals can provide meaningful relief. But if your goal is simply to move forward with your life, sometimes accepting your conviction and focusing on successful completion of your sentence is the better choice.

The decision is ultimately yours, and it should be based on your specific circumstances, goals, and resources. Whatever you decide, make sure it's an informed choice that aligns with your long-term interests.

In our final chapter, we'll explore life after conviction and the steps you can take to rebuild and move forward, regardless of whether you appeal your case.

CHAPTER 16:

LIFE AFTER CONVICTION

RECORDS AND MOVING FORWARD

Two years after her conviction, Nancy was a different person than the scared woman who had been arrested with pills in her pocket. She'd successfully completed her probation, gotten clean, and even earned a promotion at work after her nursing board allowed her to keep her license with some restrictions. The deferred adjudication was still on her record, but there was no finding of guilt and it no longer defined her life. "I thought my world was ending when this all started," Nancy reflected. "Now I realize it was actually a new beginning."

If you're reading this chapter, you've made it through the hardest part of your journey. Whether you completed probation, served your sentence, or are just starting to think about what comes next, you should be proud of how far you've come. Yes, having a criminal record creates challenges, but it doesn't have to limit your potential or destroy your dreams. Millions of Americans live successful, fulfilling lives despite having criminal convictions in their past.

Remember: This is a chapter in your story, not the final page. You are still the same person with the same talents, skills, and potential you had before this happened. A criminal charge doesn't erase your education, your work experience, your relationships, or your dreams. It adds complexity to your journey, but it doesn't end your journey.

Your conviction is part of your story, but it's not the end of your story. What matters now is what you do moving forward. You have the power to rebuild your reputation, pursue your goals, and prove that people can change and grow from their mistakes. This chapter will show you practical strategies for dealing with background checks, rebuilding your career, and taking steps to minimize the long-term impact of your conviction. Most importantly, it will remind you that your future is still entirely in your hands. You've overcome the hardest part - now it's time to build the life you want to live.

MOVING FORWARD ACTION PLAN

Immediate Priorities:

- ☐ Complete all terms of your sentence successfully
- ☐ Address any substance abuse or underlying issues
- ☐ Rebuild family and personal relationships
- ☐ Establish stable employment and housing
- ☐ Begin building positive community connections

Long-Term Goals:

- ☐ Research record sealing or expungement options
- ☐ Develop career advancement strategies
- ☐ Build savings and financial stability
- ☐ Engage in community service or advocacy
- ☐ Help others facing similar challenges

UNDERSTANDING YOUR CRIMINAL RECORD

Knowing what's on your record and how it might appear helps you plan for the future.

What Shows Up on Background Checks

Arrest Records:

- Initial arrest information
- Charges filed
- Court proceedings
- Final disposition

Conviction Information:

- Type of offense
- Date of conviction
- Sentence imposed
- Completion status

Probation Records:

- Supervision details
- Compliance history
- Successful completion
- Any violations

Types of Background Checks

Pre-Employment Screening:

- Most common type you'll encounter
- Usually covers 7-10 years
- Varies by employer and position
- Some positions require more extensive checks

Professional Licensing:

- Comprehensive criminal history
- May include arrests without convictions
- Updated when licenses renewed
- Different standards for different professions

Housing Applications:

- Landlord screening services
- Focus on recent criminal activity
- May exclude certain types of housing
- Public housing has specific rules

Financial Services:

- Credit checks often include criminal history
- Banks and financial institutions
- Insurance applications
- Loan applications

💡 DISCLOSURE STRATEGY

Honesty is almost always the best policy. Most employers and landlords appreciate upfront disclosure with context rather than discovering information later. Your explanation and rehabilitation matter more than the conviction itself.

EMPLOYMENT AFTER CONVICTION

Finding and maintaining employment is crucial for rebuilding your life.

Job Search Strategies

Target Supportive Employers:

- Companies with "second chance" hiring policies
- Small businesses where you can speak directly to decision makers
- Industries with labor shortages
- Organizations focused on rehabilitation and second chances

Emphasize Your Strengths:

- Skills and experience you bring
- Work history before your conviction
- Education and training
- Personal growth and lessons learned

Network Effectively:

- Personal and professional contacts
- Community organizations
- Religious institutions
- Recovery support groups

Handling the Application Process

"Have you ever been convicted" Questions:

- Answer honestly but strategically
- Focus on rehabilitation and growth
- Prepare a brief, positive explanation
- Emphasize current circumstances

Preparing Your Explanation:

- Take responsibility without dwelling on details
- Explain what you learned from the experience
- Describe steps you've taken to address underlying issues
- Focus on how you're different now

Timing Your Disclosure:

- Some advocate for disclosure after initial interest
- Others prefer upfront honesty
- Know your local laws about when employers can ask
- Consider the specific industry and position

Building Career Advancement

Prove Your Value:

- Exceed expectations in your performance
- Volunteer for additional responsibilities
- Develop new skills and certifications
- Build strong relationships with colleagues

Document Your Success:

- Keep records of achievements
- Collect positive performance reviews
- Gather character references
- Build a portfolio of accomplishments

Plan for Growth:

- Set realistic career goals
- Identify skills needed for advancement
- Pursue education and training opportunities
- Consider entrepreneurship if traditional employment is limited

SIDEBAR: KEY TERMS

EXPUNGEMENT:

Legal process to completely remove criminal records.

SEALING:

Restricting access to criminal records from public view.

NON-DISCLOSURE:

Texas process allowing sealing of some deferred adjudication records.

CERTIFICATE OF REHABILITATION:

Document showing successful completion of sentence and rehabilitation.

PARDON:

Executive forgiveness that may restore rights and privileges.

BAN THE BOX:

Laws restricting when employers can ask about criminal history.

FAIR CREDIT REPORTING ACT:

Federal law governing background check procedures.

COLLATERAL CONSEQUENCES:

Civil penalties and restrictions that follow criminal convictions.

HOUSING AND FINANCIAL SERVICES

Criminal records can affect housing and financial opportunities, but strategies exist to overcome these barriers.

Finding Housing

Rental Market Challenges:

- Many landlords conduct background checks
- Some automatically reject applicants with convictions
- Public housing may have restrictions
- Credit scores affected by legal costs

Strategies for Success:

- Be upfront with potential landlords
- Provide character references
- Offer larger security deposits
- Consider private landlords over large companies
- Look into housing programs for people with records

Building Rental History:

- Start with less desirable properties if necessary
- Pay rent on time and maintain property well
- Build relationships with landlords
- Work toward better housing over time

Financial Services

Banking Challenges:

- Some banks check criminal histories
- Certain convictions may limit account types
- Investment services may have restrictions
- Professional financial services careers affected

Building Financial Stability:

- Start with basic checking and savings accounts
- Use secured credit cards to rebuild credit
- Pay all bills on time
- Save consistently even if amounts are small
- Consider credit counseling if needed

Insurance Considerations:

- Auto insurance rates may be affected
- Life insurance applications ask about convictions
- Professional liability insurance may be limited
- Health insurance generally not affected

RECORD SEALING AND EXPUNGEMENT OPTIONS

Understanding your options for cleaning up your record can open new opportunities.

Texas Non-Disclosure Orders

Eligibility for Deferred Adjudication:

- Successfully completed deferred adjudication probation
- Waited required time period after completion
- No subsequent convictions
- Offense eligible for non-disclosure

Waiting Periods:

- Immediate eligibility for some misdemeanors
- 2 years for most Class A misdemeanors
- 5 years for most felonies
- Some offenses never eligible

Effect of Non-Disclosure:

- Seals records from most employers
- Law enforcement still has access
- Licensing boards may still see records
- Federal agencies retain access

Expungement Possibilities

Very Limited in Texas:

- Charges dismissed
- Acquittal at trial
- Pardoned by governor
- Identity theft cases

Complete Record Removal:

- Records destroyed by agencies
- Can legally deny arrest occurred
- No waiting periods required
- Rare for drug convictions

Pardons and Clemency

Governor's Pardon Authority:

- Can restore civil rights
- May enable record sealing
- Extremely rare
- Requires compelling circumstances

Factors Considered:

- Time since conviction
- Rehabilitation efforts
- Community service
- Character references
- Need for pardon

⚠ RECORD RELIEF REALITY

Most drug convictions cannot be sealed or expunged in Texas. Focus your energy on building a positive life and reputation rather than waiting for legal remedies that may never be available.

REBUILDING YOUR REPUTATION CHECKLIST

Personal Development:

- ☐ Complete substance abuse treatment if applicable
- ☐ Pursue education or vocational training
- ☐ Develop healthy relationships and support systems
- ☐ Engage in regular community service
- ☐ Practice consistent, responsible behavior

Professional Growth:

- ☐ Maintain steady employment
- ☐ Exceed expectations in work performance
- ☐ Develop new skills and certifications
- ☐ Build positive professional references
- ☐ Consider leadership or mentoring opportunities

Community Engagement:

- ☐ Volunteer with local organizations
- ☐ Participate in community improvement projects
- ☐ Speak about your experience if appropriate
- ☐ Mentor others facing similar challenges
- ☐ Build relationships with community leaders

REBUILDING PERSONAL RELATIONSHIPS

Criminal convictions can strain family and personal relationships, but healing is possible.

Family Relationships

Rebuilding Trust:

- Consistent, reliable behavior over time
- Open communication about your experience
- Taking responsibility without making excuses
- Following through on commitments

Addressing Hurt and Disappointment:

- Allow family members to express their feelings
- Don't minimize the impact of your actions
- Show through actions, not just words
- Be patient with the healing process

Creating New Memories:

- Focus on positive shared experiences
- Participate in family traditions and events
- Show interest in family members' lives
- Be present and engaged

Romantic Relationships

Dating Disclosure:

- When and how to share your history
- Focus on who you are now
- Allow potential partners to make informed decisions
- Don't hide information that will eventually surface

Building Healthy Relationships:

- Address any underlying issues that contributed to your conviction
- Develop good communication skills
- Practice honesty and transparency
- Work on personal growth and stability

Friendships

Choosing Positive Influences:

- Distance yourself from people who encourage illegal activity
- Build friendships with people who support your goals
- Participate in positive activities and organizations
- Be the kind of friend you want to have

Dealing with Judgment:

- Some people will judge you based on your past
- Focus on those who see your growth and potential
- Don't waste energy trying to convince everyone
- Let your actions speak louder than explanations

CONTRIBUTING TO YOUR COMMUNITY

Giving back helps rebuild your reputation and provides personal fulfillment.

Volunteer Opportunities

Organizations That Welcome People with Records:

- Recovery support organizations
- Homeless shelters and food banks
- Youth mentoring programs
- Community cleanup projects
- Religious organizations

Skills-Based Volunteering:

- Use your professional skills for nonprofit organizations
- Teach classes or workshops
- Provide technical assistance
- Mentor young people entering your field

Advocacy and Speaking:

- Share your story to help others
- Advocate for criminal justice reform
- Speak at treatment programs
- Participate in reentry programs

Professional Contributions

Mentoring Others:

- Help other people with records find employment
- Share job search strategies and resources
- Provide emotional support and encouragement

- Connect people with helpful resources

Industry Involvement:

- Participate in professional organizations
- Attend industry conferences and events
- Write articles or blog posts about your experience
- Serve on committees or boards

Community Leadership

Civic Participation:

- Attend city council or school board meetings
- Participate in community planning processes
- Join neighborhood associations
- Vote in elections if rights restored

Problem Solving:

- Identify community needs you can help address
- Organize or participate in solution-oriented projects
- Collaborate with diverse community stakeholders
- Focus on practical improvements

LONG-TERM LIFE PLANNING

Successful reintegration requires thinking strategically about your future.

Setting Realistic Goals

Short-Term (1-2 years):

- Complete all sentence requirements
- Establish stable housing and employment
- Address substance abuse or mental health issues
- Rebuild key personal relationships

Medium-Term (3-5 years):

- Advance in career or change fields
- Build financial stability and savings
- Strengthen community connections
- Consider record sealing options

Long-Term (5+ years):

- Achieve career and financial goals
- Consider homeownership
- Mentor others and give back
- Build lasting legacy of positive contributions

Financial Planning

Emergency Fund:

- Build savings for unexpected expenses
- Aim for 3-6 months of living expenses
- Start small but save consistently
- Keep funds in easily accessible accounts

Retirement Planning:

- Take advantage of employer retirement plans
- Consider IRAs if employer plans not available

- Start investing even small amounts
- Plan for long-term financial security

Insurance Needs:

- Health insurance through employer or marketplace
- Auto insurance if you drive
- Renters or homeowners insurance
- Life insurance if you have dependents

Health and Wellness

Physical Health:

- Regular medical checkups
- Healthy diet and exercise
- Avoid substance abuse
- Manage stress effectively

Mental Health:

- Continue counseling if beneficial
- Practice stress management techniques
- Build strong support networks
- Address any ongoing mental health needs

Spiritual Growth:

- Explore practices that give your life meaning
- Connect with religious or spiritual communities
- Develop sense of purpose beyond yourself
- Find ways to serve others

NANCY'S LIFE TODAY

"Five years later, I'm grateful for everything that happened. It forced me to address my addiction and made me a stronger person. I speak at treatment programs now, and I've helped several colleagues who faced similar struggles. My record is still there, but it's just one part of a much bigger story."

HELPING OTHERS AND ADVOCACY

One of the most meaningful ways to move forward is to help others facing similar challenges.

Peer Support

Recovery Programs:

- Sponsor others in 12-step programs
- Share your experience and strength
- Provide hope through example
- Connect people with resources

Reentry Support:

- Help people leaving prison or jail
- Share practical advice about employment and housing
- Provide emotional support and encouragement
- Connect people with community resources

System Reform Advocacy

Criminal Justice Reform:

- Support organizations working for reform
- Share your story with policymakers
- Advocate for better reentry programs
- Support fair hiring practices

Professional Change:

- Work to change hiring practices in your industry
- Educate employers about the value of second chances
- Advocate for professional licensing reform
- Support colleagues facing similar challenges

Public Speaking and Education

Sharing Your Story:

- Speak at treatment programs
- Address professional organizations
- Participate in community education programs
- Write about your experience

Key Messages:

- People can change and deserve second chances
- The importance of addressing underlying issues
- How support systems make a difference
- The value of redemption and forgiveness

CREATING YOUR LEGACY

Your criminal conviction doesn't have to define your legacy. You have the power to write the rest of your story.

From Mistake to Meaning

Learning and Growth:

- What did you learn from your experience?
- How are you different now than before?
- What wisdom can you share with others?
- How has adversity made you stronger?

Helping Others:

- Who can benefit from your experience?
- What unique perspective do you offer?
- How can you prevent others from making similar mistakes?
- What positive change can you create?

Building Something Lasting

Professional Excellence:

- Become known for your competence and character
- Exceed expectations consistently
- Build a reputation for reliability and integrity
- Contribute to your field in meaningful ways

Community Impact:

- Identify needs you're uniquely positioned to address
- Build programs or organizations that help others
- Create lasting positive change
- Be remembered for your contributions, not your mistakes

Family and Personal Legacy:

- Be the parent, spouse, or family member you want to be
- Create positive memories and traditions
- Model resilience and growth for others
- Show that people can overcome adversity

FREQUENTLY ASKED QUESTIONS

Q **How long will my conviction affect my life?**

A The impact decreases over time, especially with positive behavior. Many effects fade within 5-10 years, though some may be permanent.

Q **Should I tell people about my conviction?**

A Be honest when required, strategic when optional. Focus on growth and current circumstances rather than past mistakes.

Q **Can I ever get my conviction removed from my record?**

A Very rarely in Texas. Most drug convictions cannot be expunged or sealed. Focus on building a positive life despite the record.

Q **Will my conviction affect my children?**

A Generally no direct legal effects, but be prepared to explain age-appropriately and model positive behavior and growth.

Q **How do I know if I need to disclose my conviction?**

A Read applications carefully, consult with attorneys if unsure, and err on the side of honesty when the stakes are high.

YOUR NEW BEGINNING

As we reach the end of this guidebook, remember that this is really the beginning of the next chapter of your life. Your criminal conviction was a significant event, but it doesn't have to be the defining event. You have the power to shape your future through the choices you make every day.

Key Principles for Moving Forward:

Take Responsibility: Own your mistakes without making excuses, but don't let guilt paralyze you.

Focus on Growth: Use your experience as motivation to become a better person and build a better life.

Help Others: Share your experience and resources to help others avoid or overcome similar challenges.

Build Something Positive: Create value in your work, relationships, and community that outweighs past mistakes.

Be Patient: Rebuilding takes time. Trust the process and celebrate small victories along the way.

Stay Connected: Maintain relationships with people who support your growth and positive choices.

Keep Perspective: Your conviction is part of your story, but you're still writing the rest of the chapters.

The road ahead may have challenges, but you've already proven you can overcome adversity. You've survived the worst part of this process, learned valuable lessons, and developed strength you didn't know you had. Now it's time to use those lessons and that strength to build the life you want.

Your past doesn't determine your future. Your choices from this moment forward do. Make them count.

The end of your legal case is the beginning of your real life. Go live it well.

Made in the USA
Monee, IL
03 November 2026

67385370R00203